The Coming of God
Maria Boulding

First published 1982
SPCK
Holy Trinity Church
Marylebone Road
London NW1 4DU

British Library Cataloguing in Publication Data

Boulding, Maria
  The coming of God.
  1. God
  I. Title
  231   BT102

  ISBN 0-281-04009-5

Printed in Great Britain at
The Camelot Press Ltd, Southampton

Contents

Acknowledgements

Unless otherwise stated, the Scripture quotations in this publication are from the Revised Standard Version of the Bible, copyrighted 1946 and 1952 by the Division of Christian Education of the National Council of the Churches of Christ in the USA.

Thanks are due to the following for permission to quote from copyright sources:

The Oxford and Cambridge University Presses, for extracts from the New English Bible, second edition © 1970.

Darton, Longman & Todd, for extracts from the Jerusalem Bible.

The Grail, England, for extracts from *The Psalms: A New Translation*, published by Collins (1963).

Faber and Faber, for extracts from 'A Song for Simeon', 'Ash Wednesday', 'East Coker' and 'The Dry Salvages' by T. S. Eliot, published in *Collected Poems 1909–1962*; also for an extract from *Markings* by Dag Hammarskjöld, translated by W. H. Auden and Leif Sjöberg.

The Hogarth Press, for a poem from *Sonnets to Orpheus* by Rainer Maria Rilke, translated by J. B. Leishman.

Sheed and Ward, for a poem by Caryll Houselander, quoted in *Caryll Houselander* by Maisie Ward.

Dom Philip Jebb, for a previously unpublished poem.

Dom Ralph Wright, for his poem 'Messiah', first published in *Spirit and Life* by the Benedictine Convent of Perpetual Adoration, Missouri.

1 Longing for God

My soul longs for you in the night,
my spirit within me keeps vigil for you.
Isaiah 26.9

If you want God, and long for union with him, yet sometimes wonder what that means or whether it can mean anything at all, you are already walking with the God who comes. If you are at times so weary and involved with the struggle of living that you have no strength even to want him, yet are still dissatisfied that you don't, you are already keeping Advent in your life. If you have ever had an obscure intuition that the truth of things is somehow better, greater, more wonderful than you deserve or desire, that the touch of God in your life stills you by its gentleness, that there is a mercy beyond anything you could ever suspect, you are already drawn into the central mystery of salvation.

Your hope is not a mocking dream; God creates in human hearts a huge desire and a sense of need, because he wants to fill them with the gift of himself. It is because his self-sharing love is there first, forestalling any response or prayer from our side, that such hope can be in us. We cannot hope until we know, however obscurely, that there is something to hope for; if we have had no glimpse of a vision, we cannot conduct our lives with vision. And yet we do: there is hope in us, and longing, because grace was there first. God's longing for us is the spring of ours for him.

Your incurable longing for God cannot be otherwise explained. It is true that human beings need to hope as badly as they need food and oxygen, but one of the worst things about being really poor is that you do not hope; you simply fear. Millions of people in today's world are deprived of food, decent living conditions, health, opportunities and culture. They are not dynamic people, full of hopes and

1

dreams; they are too weary. Apathy, inertia and fear are part of the syndrome of poverty, and people almost forget that there can be anything better. Hope dies.

Many people in the 'developed' countries are in similar case, but the poverty is spiritual. If men and women have no vision, can see no meaning in their lives, are conscious that our civilization has lost its way and doubt whether there is any future for their children, they are not dynamic either. They do not live on hopes and dreams. They too are apathetic, though they have certain escape routes from their emptiness which are not available to the materially poor. And yet, with so much telling against it, you are longing for God. You are not alone.

Modern man has discovered his place in time, and one of the effects of this is to show us how old the longing is. We are aware of the immense ages of prehistory, and have some idea of the long procession of our fellow human beings who lived and died without leaving a trace or a word to us, their heirs, during the millennia before man learnt to leave a message, to record for posterity what was in his heart. Yet as soon as people are able to communicate across the genera-tions, they tell us in various ways of a universal thirst: a search for happiness, for meaning, for peace, for life after death, for the beyond. Under many strange forms, there is a longing for the unknown God.

Unknown, but only up to a point. The hope would not have been there if mankind had been without him; grace awakened the longing. Creation is shot through with the self-gift of God. The divine life, the divine self-giving called grace, is the secret dynamism at the heart of creation, penetrating, lifting and inspiring it from the innermost personal core of every human being, drawing it onwards to its destiny. Grace is the initiative of God, his self-offer that is prior to any kind of movement towards him by the creature. It is sheer gift, bestowed wherever human beings do not finally close themselves against him and refuse his love.

The gift of God is for the poor, the needy, the empty. It is for those who are too poor to recognize or identify their need. It is for those who do know their need, and hunger and thirst for him. It is for those who do not even suspect the depth of tenderness with which they are loved, yet are potentially open. God is most known as God when he gives to the undeserving, when he fills the hungry with good things, lifts up the downtrodden, transforms hopeless situations and brings life out of death. His gift is most typically not the crowning of our achievements, but wealth for the bankrupt and power at the service of the weak. When human resources are missing but people are open to God, then is the moment of faith, then God's desire to give meets human receptivity unhindered.

That characteristic pattern of divine self-giving is the central theme of this book. It will crop up variously in the chapters that follow, but there are three instances of it which must be looked at briefly now, because they will concern us throughout, three spheres of experience and faith where the gift of God comes to the poor. The first is the story of Israel's longing as recorded in the Old Testament, an emptiness and a need which were met by God's flesh-taking in Christ. The second is our own experience of spiritual poverty which is met by the gift of grace, leading us on to contemplation. The third, which unites the first two through symbol and poetry, is the Christian Church's celebration of the Advent of the Lord.

No part of the universal longing of mankind can be vain, mocking or doomed to frustration, because it is God who created human beings like that, intending to be himself their absolute fulfilment. Nevertheless, the ancient world needed, as the modern world in its own way still needs, special places where the longing would be conscious and explicit, to focus the longing of the whole. Israel was such a privileged place. The chosen people were created to be a centre of attunement, receptivity and expectation, a place of felt need and desire. They were to listen to God's word, to long for him, and to be the womb-community which would bring forth the One who was to come.

Israel was a small, fairly backward and politically insig-nificant people for most of its history during the last two

3

millennia before Christ, but it was a people created to hope. It existed only because God's word of promise had called it into being, and because he was constantly entrusting himself to his Hebrew children in love. Their whole business was to listen to his word, and to respond to him in faith, obedience and worship. They should have been focusing all mankind's desire for God, but generally they did not. Their history was a faltering, stumbling progress towards an encounter, a confused and many-sided experience, often stained with sin and seldom characterized by consciousness of their orientation to God. People lived and loved, fought and traded, married and reared children, planted and built, pursuing immediate ends and the normal business of mankind. Occasionally, through the prophets and psalmists who articulated the deepest intuitions of their people, the longing would surface:

> O God, you are my God, for you I long;
> for you my soul is thirsting.
> (Ps. 63 (62).2, Grail)

Not man's feeble, fickle desire for God, but God's faithful love for man shaped the history. He bound his people to himself by covenanted love, and sent prophet after prophet to kindle their hope. The Israelite prophets were men (and a few women) chosen and called by God, entrusted with his words and sent to speak them to the people. A prophet was someone who listened, embodying in himself the vocation of a people created to listen to God but often deaf. The word of the Lord, powerful and charged with divine authority, grasped him urgently, overcame his weakness, and recalled his hearers to the essentials of their covenant relationship with Yahweh, the Lord. Always it was a contemporary word, addressed to an actual situation, but because it was also the word of the Lord, whose plans spanned the centuries, it often had a meaning deeper than either speaker or hearers could fully grasp.

To the Israelites a 'word' was more than a sound conveying meaning; it could also be a powerful creative deed. There was an interlocking of saving act with prophetic message:

victory or disaster or any other event in their experience
would be foretold and interpreted by a prophet, and the
appropriate response demanded. Both message and event
were Yahweh's 'word' to his people. Under the pressure of
history and experience, and through this revealing word, the
chosen people came to see God's saving interventions in the
past as pledges for the future. They hoped for a new Son of
David, a great Prophet like Moses, a mysterious Servant of
the Lord who would gather Israel but also be a light to the
nations, a Son of Man who, though human, was to come
down from heaven. The future hope was complex, and
necessarily conditioned by the particular experiences of a
people frequently endangered and extremely interested in
survival and material prosperity.

Praying, hoping, suffering and learning, the nameless
poor people of Israel lived through this history, discovering
through their powerlessness and lack of material supports a
call to be open to God. These poor were the spiritual élite of
the nation, the contrite and humble, and to them the future
belonged. In a school of hardship they learned how to cling
to the most spiritual and durable elements in God's promises, and they waited in confidence for the consolation of
Israel. The little group in the first two chapters of Luke's
Gospel are typical of these poor, and it is they who welcome
Jesus at his coming: Zechariah and Elizabeth, Simeon and
Anna, Joseph and Mary.

In the last, expectant years before Christ, Israel was
pregnant with salvation. A late passage found in the Book of
Isaiah evokes poignantly its failed childbearing:

> Like a woman with child,
> who writhes and cries out in her pangs,
> when she is near her time,
> so were we because of thee, O Lord;
> we were with child, we writhed,
> we have as it were brought forth wind.
> We have wrought no deliverance in the earth.[1]

This could have been the end of the story: a miscarriage.
But it was not. Where the poor were waiting, hoping,

humbly praying and listening, where human resources were at zero but there was unconditional faith, God worked his wonders. Mary was powerless and poor, but she listened to the word of God at the heart of a people who should have listened; she welcomed the word and gave it life within her life. Before the Word became flesh in her womb, she conceived the Word of God in her spirit, as the Christian Fathers delighted to say. In her there was an emptiness that was active receptivity; there was faith and obedience, a welcome to God. The word to Israel had been both message and saving event; Mary believed this new message and acted with energy and intelligence within this new saving event. But now the Word was also a Person, her child, and she dedicated herself with her whole being to his service.

One of the most striking things about the Old Testament story is that, whatever the follies and betrayals of the human beings who had been involved with it down the centuries, all things were worked together for good by God who willed to give himself. The lifelines that give unity and movement to the story emerged from human experience and the necessities of living; particularly is this true of the line of hope associated with David's dynasty. Yet they were also God-given, God-directed. People blundered and stumbled, sinned or co-operated only half-heartedly; never could anyone know more than his own small role in a complex affair, his own circumscribed response to God's particular call. They walked and watched in the dark, even though it may not usually have felt like that. They kept a long night vigil until salvation dawned in Christ, a centuries-long Advent, a watch on behalf of the whole family of mankind.

In Israel's vigil the world also shares, because it epitomizes a perennial human experience. Our poverty of spirit, our darkness and confusion, our need and thirst, are part of the world's Advent and the Advent of our lives. They are not sheer negativity; they cry out to God. Thirst is an experience of water. There is a discontent in us that can be partly stifled by material satisfactions, but some experiences tend to awaken it. It may be roused by beauty, or by love, by great pain or by the nearness of death. It can surface easily in times of silence when we try to confront the mystery of ourselves and wonder about God.

If you have ever known this discontent and pondered the mysteries and contradictions of the human condition, it is of consequence to both yourself and others that you hope, expect and listen in silence to the word of God who is himself attuning you to hear. Your silent listening through prayer, through people and through events will be very personal; it may seem very solitary, but it is not. You are the answering readiness, the receptivity, without which even today God cannot give as he longs to give. Our noisy, busy world has little time to listen and wait; and – what is worse – it is starved of hope. So many hopes disappoint, and people are afraid of being disappointed yet again. It is when we reach the brink of despair that hope grounded in God has a chance, because there is nothing else left. The modern world can surely not be far from the brink.

In the name of very many other people you can listen to the word that tells you you are unconditionally loved. The monotony and drabness of life is no block; the failure that our prayer seems to be and the ambiguous mixture in most of our choices are all part of it. Just as all the vicissitudes of Israel's history were working together for good towards that unheard-of gift of love, so it is with your personal history: all the lifelines of your experience are built in by God. All your hopes and disappointments, your joy and suffering, your achievement and failure, your ups and downs: none of it is wasted. Provided only that you consent, and hold to that consent without qualification, the work of grace is going on in you through the whole business of living, to hollow you out, to make you *capax Dei* as the old mystics used to say, able to receive God. You yourself are the place of desire and need. All your love, your stretching out, your hope, your thirst, God is creating in you so that he may fill you. It is not your desire that makes it happen, but his. He longs through your heart. Your insufficiency and your forgetting to long for him are

7

no barrier. In your prayer God is seeking you and himself creating the prayer; he is on the inside of the longing.

> When God at first made man,
> Having a glasse of blessings standing by;
> Let us, said he, poure on him all we can:
> Let the world's riches, which dispersed lie,
> > Contract into a span.
>
> So strength first made a way;
> Then beautie flow'd, then wisdome, honour, pleasure:
> When almost all was out, God made a stay,
> Perceiving that alone of all his treasure
> > Rest in the bottome lay.
>
> For if I should, said he,
> Bestow this jewell also on my creature,
> He would adore my gifts in stead of me,
> And rest in Nature, not the God of Nature.
> > So both should losers be.
>
> Yet let him keep the rest,
> But keep them with repining restlessnesse:
> Let him be rich and wearie, that at least,
> If goodnesse leade him not, yet wearinesse
> > May tosse him to my breast.[2]

Our desire for union and our longing for God are already his gift. Because he longs to give himself to us, because his glory is not isolation but self-giving love, he creates in human beings the capacity to receive him. The longing is in us because he creates it in us, and he creates it because he wants to fill us and satisfy us with that which 'eye has not seen, nor ear heard, nor heart of man conceived'.

Every year in the weeks before Christmas the Christian Church celebrates the season called Advent, the Coming of the Lord. It is a poetic, mysterious and very beautiful time, during which the prayers and longings of prophets and psalmists and anonymous poor people of the Old Testament come into their own. We are invited to identify with the people who waited for Christ during that long night watch, and certainly the poetic elements, combined with the darkness and stars for those who live in the north, make it easy. Nevertheless, we could be dogged by a feeling of unreality, a suspicion that there is something artificial about pretending to look forward to Christ's coming when we know that he has come already.

He has come, certainly, and that historic moment of his human birth cannot be repeated. The clock cannot be put back. The first Christmas was a gift from God which has changed human life and history, inserting into the heart of our affairs the love which gives them meaning. But the Advent we keep is not a poetic make-believe, or a nostalgic historical pageant, or even an exercise in remembering our roots, although this might have value. The coming of God in Christ still continues, and will be consummated in a coming and a gift beyond the stretch of our hope. We are an Advent people. The season of Advent celebrates in symbolic form a reality of our own lives and of all men's destiny with God, because he who came in weakness at Bethlehem is he who will come again.

Constantly he comes. He came as a man into our human situation, accepted human experience as his own and lived it through to the bitter end, in order that what was bitter might be turned into sweetness and human experience become an expression of his sacrificial, redeeming love. He has transformed it from the inside, and offered us the possibility of allowing him to transform it in our lives too. The one historical, unique birth at Bethlehem makes possible his birth in the many lives of those who will receive him, to whom he gives the power to become children of God. He is born in us continually as our minds, our actions, our reactions, our relationships, our experience and our prayer are Christified. But this is a lifetime's task, and we need to pray constantly from the still pre-Christian areas in us, 'Come, Lord Jesus'.

He will come again in glory. As he accepted a human body, a human mind, and the whole project of being a man, so he immersed himself, as we are all immersed, in human history. Henceforth it is his, and his secret grace pervades it,

9

as his grace also pervades the history of each person. The human family as a whole is oriented towards the Father, who has irrevocably said 'Yes' to it in Christ. Through its manifold, immensely complex experiences, its failures and betrayals notwithstanding, through the night of its ignorance and forgetfulness, humankind is on the way to an encounter. Those who believe that Christ will come again to claim all his brethren, those who know even a little of his comings in their own lives, are not alien to all the others. In them the welcome, the longing, the faith and hope are explicit, but explicit for the sake of all who in sincerity of heart look for the God who is and who was and who is to come.

The particular experience of the chosen people, Israel, was like a sacrament, a symbolic expression created by God of the response and readiness that he needed in order to make his ultimate gift. In Israel the long preparation of mankind was focused. This is why we are invited to identify with Israel-the-symbol during the annual celebration of Advent. What is being expressed in this symbolic way is a reality of human life, and human life not simply for a special season of a few weeks each year, but all the time. Our lives are an Advent, a time of waiting, listening and hoping, a time of openness to the unimaginable gift of God. Israel was a focus; the Christian Church is a focus. But so are you.

The liturgy of Advent plays with certain themes of hope and promise which were vital elements in the experience of the Old Testament people. By praying, suffering and living out these themes, Israel learned to know God. They converge towards Christ and are fufilled in him, but with an unexpected twist and a transposition to a new depth of meaning. The coming of the Word made flesh was not an end to the story but a new beginning, and so the same themes of expectancy are part of our experience too, whether in our personal prayer and life with God, or in the corporate life of the Church and the human family, or both. By praying and living through these experiences we too can learn to know him, and to recognize and welcome the coming of God that our world sorely needs.

Such are the convictions of which this book is born. Chapter 2 considers the risks and challenges of living in response to the promises of God, and the characteristic mode of his giving where situations seem hopeless. The next two chapters dwell on wintry aspects of the waiting, and the springlike quality of Christ's birth as man and of our new birth in him. This leads into a pivotal chapter on listening to God's word, which was Israel's business but could not be achieved until the coming of Christ who was both Word and Listener; this fifth chapter is central to the book, and indeed the book itself is an attempt to listen to the Word. Chapter 6 explores a theme closely related to the Word and prominent in Advent, that of personified Wisdom active in creation. Christ is the Wisdom of God and his redeeming work is a new creation. Chapter 7 considers how he achieves it as the humbled Servant who does not seek his own glory, and how his destiny is bound up with Jerusalem, the city to which the promises of glory were given. The mystery of the God who comes is dwelt on in Chapter 8: who is he? Israel asked the question, and so do we; though his comings truly reveal him they never exhaust his mystery, and the Church lives with it, contemplating. All our experience of his coming and his gifts are leading us towards a final coming, which is the subject of Chapter 9. Advent is the sacrament of Everyman's search.

11

2 The Risk of Promise

All which I took from thee I did but take,
          Not for thy harms,
But just that thou might'st seek it in My arms.
      All which thy child's mistake
Fancies as lost, I have stored for thee at home:
      Rise, clasp My hand, and come![1]

Disappointment is one of the most negative of human experiences. It is a terrible thing to see hope and joy die in a child's eyes as a bitter realization dawns. It may be even worse to see settled, dull disillusionment in the eyes of an adult who has been disappointed by life so often that he or she has given up hope as altogether too painful. Hope is a dynamism, a source of strength for the weary; it keeps us going as it sustained Israel through the long march of the Old Testament to the moment of God's ultimate self-giving in Christ. God gave them lifelines of hope, and their spirits lived on his promises. Yet a most remarkable feature of their history is that it can also be read as a story of disappointment.

Disappointment, strangely, did not suffocate their hope but strengthened it. They lived on promise, but grew through disappointment towards a purer hope, a hope less unworthy of the God who loved them. It was not a serene, predictable kind of growth, but a series of risky leaps. From time to time a representative person or group was asked by God to let go of a pattern of living which not only meant material security but had been the setting in which they knew his presence. Every time it was like dying to an older order of things and being born anew. To make this point clear we shall have to recall the outlines of the story.

God's promise to Abraham was the foundational hope. 'Go from your country and your kindred and your father's house to the land that I will show you. And I will make of you a great nation. . . . And by you all the families of the earth shall bless themselves' (Gen. 12.1–3). There was a double focus in this promise: possession of the land of Canaan, and posterity for an elderly man who had no heir. Abraham believed. Whatever the circumstances and the psychological pathways through which the word had come to him, he had no doubt that he had met God. Beyond the limitations imposed by custom, habit, an inherited way of life and Abraham's own imperfect understanding, stood someone who offered and requested friendship. Abraham took the other at his word, broke through the limitations and obeyed. He entrusted himself and his future to God, and waited in hope for the dream to come true.

The land and descendants were given to him, but it was all precarious. He and his immediate heirs were merely sojourners; the only legal stake he had in the land was a piece large enough for a grave. At the climax of his friendship with God he was asked to destroy the child born to him of promise and long waiting, the child on whose fragile life the meaning of his whole relationship with God depended. He obeyed, though at the last moment his hand was held. Beyond all reason he had been willing to trust God, and to let go of what seemed to be the only way of securing the future: to let go, as it seemed, of the promise itself, simply because the one whom he loved was asking it. He walked in newness of life as God's friend, and the future, paradoxically, was thereby assured.

Famine forced Abraham's posterity to leave the land of promise and settle in Egypt. After some hundreds of years God spoke again, promising through Moses that he would lead them out of slavery and give them the land flowing with milk and honey, as he had sworn to their fathers. Moses believed. The people believed, for the moment, and Yahweh snatched them from Egypt with a strong hand and an outstretched arm. He cared for them in the desert, and bound them to himself in a covenant of love. Yet the demand made on them was great; Egypt had offered security, even if it was the security of slaves, and this open-ended adventure

13

with the mysterious God of the wilderness was terrifying. It meant breaking away from all that was familiar, both materially and spiritually, into a new life, and they often wanted to withdraw. Through a searing experience of poverty and temptation they learnt to know Yahweh's faithfulness. It was a precious time, their own sinfulness notwithstanding, and the memory of it was a pledge of hope in every situation of weakness and need that they would know later.

Under Joshua's leadership they entered the land, because Yahweh their God fought for them. Considerable disillusionment followed, for the land was beset by powerful enemies, and their own weakness, both military and moral, was amply demonstrated. Eventually they gained stability under a king, and at the end of the eleventh century BC a new era opened with David's reign.

David was the man whom Yahweh had chosen and advanced to power, and to him the promise was explicitly renewed. It was focused now in the permanence of the Davidic dynasty:

> The Lord will make you a house. . . . I will raise up your offspring after you . . . and I will establish his kingdom. He shall build a house for my name, and I will establish the throne of his kingdom for ever. I will be his father, and he shall be my son. . . . I will not take my steadfast love from him. . . . Your house and your kingdom shall be made sure for ever before me; your throne shall be established for ever. (2 Sam. 7.11–16)

Nothing, it seemed, could be clearer: the future of Israel, and in some sense the future of the nations, whose salvation had also been implied in the old promise to Abraham, were now bound up with the monarchy and with the family of David. It was hinted that a 'son' of David would be the bearer of salvation. As David went from strength to strength, putting Israel on the map as a minor empire, the future seemed secure. The promises were on the way to realization; Israel was prosperous. Under his son Solomon a temple of unprecedented beauty and wealth was built to the glory of

Yahweh, who honoured it with signs of his indwelling. Security, permanence, power, achievement . . . they had localized the God of the promises, and very nearly domesticated him.

It was a brittle achievement. The kingdom split in two soon afterwards, leaving to David's heirs sovereignty over the smaller southern part only, the kingdom of Judah with its capital at Jerusalem. The northern kingdom, which kept the hallowed name 'Israel', went its own way, and succumbed to the superpower, Assyria, some two centuries later. Judah survived, precariously, but in the sixth century BC it too was engulfed by the new superpower, Babylon. Jerusalem, God's holy city, fell to the Gentile armies, the temple was destroyed and the flower of the nation deported. God's people was wiped off the map.

The exile was the greatest disaster they had ever suffered; it was crushing and horrifying not simply in the way that war always is for prisoners and refugees, but because it seemed to call in question the whole meaning and validity of their faith. The problem was not whether they had deserved this catastrophe, for the prophets had never tired of pointing out to them that they had. The central question for faith was rather how to hold on to the conviction of God's faithfulness to his promises – a faithfulness which surely could not be turned aside for ever by Israel's sin – when all the signs that had guaranteed it were destroyed. The monarchy, the temple, the feasts and sacrifices and the very land he had promised to their fathers were lost to them; all the material supports for faith were swept away. Amid the ruins of the holy city poets mourned, yet hoped:

> Remember, O remember,
> and stoop down to me. . . .
> The Lord's true love is surely not spent,
> nor has his compassion failed;
> they are new every morning,
> so great is his constancy.
> The Lord, I say, is all that I have;
> therefore I will wait for him patiently.
> (Lam. 3.20, 22–4, NEB)

15

Through Jeremiah and Ezekiel God spoke to this afflicted generation, calling them to a leap of faith, offering the possibility of a new relationship with him and a new discovery of his love. The temple and the Ark of the Covenant were gone, but 'Though I scattered them among the countries, yet I have been a sanctuary to them for a while in the countries where they have gone' (Ezek. 11.16). His presence was to be found anew in their own hearts. The old covenant had been violated from their side, but through the same prophets the Lord promised a new covenant in men's hearts, marked by the forgiveness of all their sins.

In exile, grappling with the greatest disappointment of their history, God's people was challenged to be born anew, to a new hope. They pondered and prayed over the traditions of their exodus from Egypt so long ago, and their covenant-making with God in the desert. He had done the impossible thing before, and he could do it again. Second Isaiah, a prophet with the exiles,[2] sang of a way home, a glorious restoration, a purified and beautiful Jerusalem forgiven and reconciled with the Lord in a new marriage bond, and a vindication of his sovereignty over history. The same prophet also spoke of a Servant of the Lord, sometimes identified with Israel but sometimes charged with a mission to Israel, through whom the saving work of the Lord would be accomplished, at great cost in suffering for the Servant. The whole picture was not unified, and these prophecies about the Servant were variously understood, but a chastened people broke through to a new hope.

Disappointment was waiting again. They returned indeed, but to something of an anticlimax. The land fit for heroes to live in proved to be a land in which only heroes could live. They were poor, and the country was in a depressed condition. They no longer had political power or national sovereignty, and they were harassed in their attempts at reconstruction by their Samaritan neighbours. The temple was laboriously rebuilt, but 'many of the priests and Levites and heads of families, who were old enough to have seen the former house, wept and wailed aloud when they saw the foundation of this house laid' (Ezra 3.12, NEB).

16

Despite all this, hope grew stronger in the centuries that followed. It was not a vague general optimism about the future, but faith in the saving will and fidelity of God. It was still focused on David's line; psalmists and historians continued to remember that promise and to look for salvation through a new David, even though there was no longer any monarchy to give it substance. Other currents of hope flowed too: Israel looked for a Great Prophet, a Servant of the Lord, one like a Son of Man who would come with sovereignty from heaven. These centuries after the return from exile were spiritually fruitful, a time of prayer, of reflection on the lessons of the past, and of exposure to foreign cultures which helped Israel to formulate its own unique faith. They believed that 'not one of all the good promises which the Lord had made to the house of Israel had failed' (Josh. 21.45). Through humiliation and disaster, through the relentless sifting which had left only a remnant of the people as heir to the promises, they had survived to welcome a saving intervention of God which could not now be long delayed.

This story of Israel's hope is a story not of smooth progress but of successive breakthroughs. God's promise had been made to the people through Abraham, Moses, David, or one of the prophets. It had taken the concrete form of some assurance about the land, about victory, survival or repatriation, about Israel's role with regard to the Gentiles, or about the 'Day of the Lord' when peace and righteousness would reign and abundant harvests would be a sign of his blessing. Each time someone, or some people, had been asked to make a leap of faith and love in response to the one who promised, to break through a barrier, to be reborn to a new possibility. The result was fuller life, a new level and sphere of existence, but at the cost of everything on this side of the barrier. It always meant a letting go, a dying to something that had been familiar, controllable, perhaps even perfect of its kind. The clearest case is that of Abraham who, though childless, had been prosperous and secure in Ur of the Chaldees before God called him into friendship. God said, 'Come'. Abraham

17

said 'Yes' to God, and he walked in newness of life; as an old man he was new-born. But the new life was full of risk and bafflement. At a later stage, when he had been rewarded and was safe in his expectations of the future, because God had given him the promised child, he was commanded to destroy the very bearer of meaning in his adventure with God, and

> he who had received the promises was ready to offer up his only son, of whom it was said, 'Through Isaac shall your descendants be named.' He considered that God was able to raise men even from the dead.
>
> (Heb. 11.19)

St Paul makes the point clearly: Abraham's faith was a first sketch, far-off but genuine, of Christian faith in God who has raised Christ from the dead:

> In hope he believed against hope, that he should become the father of many nations. . . . He did not weaken in faith when he considered his own body, which was as good as dead because he was about a hundred years old, or when he considered the barrenness of Sarah's womb. No distrust made him waver concerning the promise of God, but he grew strong in his faith as he gave glory to God, fully convinced that God was able to do what he had promised. That is why his faith was 'reckoned to him as righteousness.' But the words, 'it was reckoned to him,' were written not for his sake alone, but for ours also. It will be reckoned to us who believe in him that raised from the dead Jesus our Lord.
>
> (Rom. 4.18–22, 24)

Our God is the God who transforms hopeless situations, and so there were fulfilments: Abraham's son, the entry into the land under Joshua, the establishment of David's throne and the return from exile. Each time God, the obscurely known Lover, said, 'Come', and Israel made a creative breakthrough to much greater possibilities than had been known before, but it was made in pain. These new beginnings were pure gift where human resources were lacking, yet they demanded a sacrificial letting-go by those who knew the love that called them. A new synthesis would result, a fuller life, and yet time and again there would be disappointment, as though God were saying, 'Not this, not this . . .', as though he were putting pressure on them to come further. The successive realizations of the promise were like sacramental signs: each was the bearer of God's love and salvation for a time, until he called his people to go through it to the reality beyond itself. At an early stage in their history he had forbidden them images which could become idols, and the continual disappointments were part of the same policy. God is always greater than anything his promises can encapsulate in a formula or give as a token, and what he was giving was himself. The disappointments were functional. In the eighth century BC Isaiah of Jerusalem expressed it in a sentence which sums up a good deal of the story: 'I will wait for the Lord, who is hiding his face from the house of Jacob, and I will hope in him' (Isa. 8.17).

The God who called and promised is the living God who gives life by passionately loving and summoning the often bewildered creature to answering love. Old patterns break as the creature responds. We know it from our own experience. Growth often proceeds in jumps, separated by quieter periods in which the new thing is assimilated, rather than in a smooth, steady line. The moments of breakthrough can be ruthlessly demanding. If the demand is refused, we do not merely continue at the old level, but shrink and shrivel into death; so we lose what we had in any case. It is an exhausting business for the tiny chicken to chip its way out of the egg, but the alternative is worse.

Again, a baby may be fast and efficient at crawling, but he becomes aware of a call to abandon this safe method of locomotion and totter on unsteady legs; it is far more precarious but it opens up considerable new possibilities. In making this painful choice the child is recapitulating that made by our distant pre-human ancestors in favour of bipedalism. What precisely provoked this change is not known for certain, but we do know what it meant. Along with freed hands and alterations in the skeleton went development of the brain and stereoscopic vision. The

19

upright creature was on its way towards a destiny of which it had no inkling; the greatest breakthrough since the emergence of life was waiting for it. One day, somewhere, one or many of them broke through another barrier, and consciousness was born.[3]

Life grows, multiplies, diversifies and joins in the dance of creation when those who live do not clutch it to themselves but let go, take risks and surrender themselves in a self-gift that is a kind of dying. In the world of the spirit it is the same: 'Unless a grain of wheat falls into the earth and dies, it remains alone; but if it dies, it bears much fruit. He who loves his life loses it, and he who hates his life in this world will keep it for eternal life' (John 12.24–5). Faith is like this. The believer lets go of human securities to entrust himself or herself into the hands of an obscurely known Lover, and there is great unknowing and the sense of risk and loss. This is true not only of the initial breakthrough when a person is born into faith; growth in the life of faith demands a constant willingness to let go and leap again. Prayer is not always a smooth, peaceful progress, but a series of detachments from everything, however spiritual and meaningful, that is not God. Like the Israelites, we are prone to idolatry, and in the lives of people who pray the idols tend to be of a refined and sophisticated character. Prayer itself can be an idol, and so can a spiritual self-image. We are loved passionately by a jealous God, and he pulls us free from them. It feels like a progressive impoverishment. Speaking to Nicodemus of the life God offers, Jesus warned him of the narrow door, the barrier to be broken through: 'Unless a man is born anew, he cannot see the kingdom of God.'[4]

Indeed, birth is the best analogy we have; perhaps death might be a better one still, but as we are on the wrong side of that breakthrough the data are not all available for inspection. Ante-natal life is very limited, but it is all the foetus knows. Were we conscious and free to choose at the time, perhaps few would have the courage to be born. It would be terrifying to be torn away from an environment and a sphere of being in which you were warm, secure and well adjusted, where all your needs were taken care of, to be thrust out into a huge, cold, noisy, alien and bewildering world, potentially hostile and dangerous, in which the first thing that happens to you is the traumatic experience of learning to breathe.

You cannot give life to others unless you have yourself painfully consented to life many times, unless you have let go of the lesser life you had and made the dangerous leap towards the love that stands beyond the barriers which would close you in on yourself. Because Israel was the womb-community, which existed in order to bring forth the Messiah, it was constantly called to be itself born anew, often in fear and pain, during the long period of preparation. There may have been many in Israel who refused to let go, but always there were some who consented to die to the old sphere of existence and to the earlier gains, and be born again into God's life. Because a remnant had always said 'Yes', life went on, and there were new openings to God's future.

Undoubtedly the prophets were among those who consented, learning the ways of God through personal anguish and direct communion with the Beyond who called. This is notably true of Hosea and Jeremiah. The hard and hidden choices must have been made too in the lives of innumerable ordinary men and women who prayed, pondered and listened to God; some of their search has been recorded for us in the psalms. But there is one current of special importance, the spiritual tradition of the 'anawim, Yahweh's poor.[5] The cry of the poor is the purest and truest voice in the chorus of prayer that articulated Israel's longing for God.

These 'anawim appear as the spiritual kernel of the nation from the seventh century BC:

> I will leave in the midst of you a people humble and lowly.
> They shall seek refuge in the name of the Lord.
> (Zeph. 3.12)

They were the have-nots, the underprivileged, the powerless, the oppressed, the people whose economic poverty drove them to unlimited trust in God. The poor man had no human vindicator, no human prospects, no reliance except the Lord who had declared himself the poor man's champion: 'If he cries to me, I will hear, for I am compassionate.'[6]

21

These especially were the people who were forced to grapple with the enigma of suffering, for the usual doctrine of prosperity for the good and disaster as punishment for the wicked did not ring true for them. Some of the probing into this problem is found in the Book of Job: its hero, overtaken by every kind of calamity, protests at the insufficiency of the simplistic solutions offered by his 'orthodox' friends, and repeatedly demands a confrontation with God so that he can put his case. In the end he gets the confrontation, but it is not the vindication he expected. His questions are not answered but simply seen to be irrelevant, as Job falls silent and worships before the mystery of God. There is a contemplative poverty. The profundity of this book's message, and the different but even more vital contribution of the Songs of the Suffering Servant in the later parts of Isaiah, must have spoken powerfully to the nameless poor of Israel. Their own afflictions, setbacks and disappointments opened them up to God in trust and intimacy; the 'intolerable wrestle with words and meanings'[7] was theirs.

The leap of self-transcendence, the responsive self-giving to the Lover who invites, is always daunting, for the poor no less than the rich; it is self-surrender in faith 'costing not less than everything'. Yet the poor have a certain advantage. As in the evolution of living things, a creative breakthrough occurs when a species is under pressure and its ways of coping with the environment are no longer adequate, so the poor of Israel were pressurized by disappointment. They bore the brunt; they could not rest satisfied with partial fulfilments from which they were in any case excluded. 'Poverty' shifted in meaning; from being an economic and social condition it became a spiritual attitude. The poor were the humble, the people who were obedient to the will of God, those whose very misery had forced their hearts open to him:

> The Lord, I say, is all that I have;
> therefore I will wait for him patiently.
> (Lam. 3.24, NEB)

Through the long night of vigil Yaweh's poor waited, hoped and humbly prayed:

I rise before dawn and cry for help,
I hope in your word.
My eyes watch through the night
to ponder your promise.
(Ps. 119 (118). 147–8, Grail)

They were not disappointed. When the Messiah came, he came very poor, so that he would be accessible to the poor of heart. Only they, who through disappointment and faith had grown beyond what was merely temporal and material in the promises, only they were ready to let go of preconceptions and recognize him. Only they were ready to receive a Saviour, because they knew they needed one.

Attuned to him as was no one else, at his coming, throughout his life and in his passover, was Mary. She was the fine flower of the *'anawim* tradition, who summed up in her own faith and availability to God the purest and strongest expectation of Israel. The Gospels of Luke and John present her as the woman of faith who stood for God's people at the all-important moment to which its history had been moving. Luke's first two chapters are a tissue of Old Testament allusions, playing on the echoes in order to bring out the full significance of Jesus's birth.[8]

'Rejoice', says the angel to Mary at the Annunciation, echoing the note of messianic joy struck by the prophet Zephaniah, who had spoken to the 'people humble and lowly' whom the Lord would cherish in Israel:

Sing aloud, O daughter of Zion. . . .
Rejoice and exult with all your heart,
O daughter of Jerusalem! . . .
The King of Israel, the Lord, is in your midst.
(Zeph. 3.14–15)

Mary is presented as the Daughter of Zion, as Israel at the moment of its highest responsiveness to God, as the place where salvation will be revealed. The lifelines of hope converge in her and in the promise she receives. Her child is to inherit the throne of his father David, and will reign for ever; the angel's words recall the prophecy of Nathan to

23

David concerning the permanence of his dynasty. The power of the Most High will 'overshadow' Mary, as in the Old Testament the cloud was the sign of Yahweh's presence and his glory filled the tabernacle from within. As a confirming sign, Mary is told of the unlooked-for conception of a son by her cousin Elizabeth, for 'nothing is impossible with God'; the words echo Genesis 18.14 where an angelic visitor, having promised a son to the elderly couple. Abraham and Sarah, meets Sarah's scepticism with the question, 'Is anything too hard for Yahweh?' Mary is like the new Ark of the Covenant, the place of God's dwelling with his people, and when she visits Elizabeth the unborn John 'leaps', as David had leaped and danced before the Ark. Mary's child is to be called Jesus, a name which corresponds to Joshua, 'Yahweh saves'.

All this is beautiful, and we may well stand back and marvel. Nothing has been wasted or lost, all the agonies and disappointments have been worth while. The overarching wisdom of God has carried the plan through, and now the Messiah for whom Israel longed is to be welcomed by this poor, silent, humble girl who represents her people. Such a reading is wholly legitimate, indeed necessary; it is what the evangelist intends, but it is important to remember that we read, as Luke wrote, with benefit of hindsight. In the full light of Easter and Pentecost and the Church's pondering of the mystery of Christ, Luke could write the Annunciation story in this poetic, allusive, theologically developed way, and we can rejoice in it, but to the people within the story it did not look like that.

As the poor and faithful of Israel had said 'Yes' to God in anguish of spirit, not seeing how things could work out but conscious only of the tearing away from what had gone before and the venture forward into the dark unknown at God's word, so Mary was being asked to make the leap of faith in response to God's self-offer and invitation. There were no models for understanding, no comforting precedents, because this thing had never happened before. The flesh-taking of the Son of God was much more than a fulfilment of Israel's expectations, much more than a satisfactory tying-up of all the strands of hope; it was the unheard-of gift, the breaking in of the wholly new thing.

Like the prophets and the anonymous believers before her, she let go of familiar, intelligible patterns and ways of relating to God and the universe, of those frameworks which had genuinely supported meaning hitherto, and were indeed God-given. She said her 'Yes' to the Beyond, she let go of her securities, faced the misunderstanding, bore the shame, accepted her own bewilderment and risk.[9] She was herself reborn to a new existence, that she might bring forth life for many. There was joy for her, and in newness of life she danced with the Beyond that was within.

3 Winters of the Spirit

O radiant Dayspring,
Splendour of eternal light and Sun of Righteousness,
come
and shine on those who dwell in darkness
and the shadow of death.[1]

It had better be said at once that this chapter* is written with the northern hemisphere principally in mind. God must make special compensatory provision for his southern children, for it is evident that the marriage between the seasons and the mysteries of Christ was solemnized in the north. As the explosion of new life in spring proclaims the Easter life that has been through death, so does the cold darkness of the northern winter in its own way reveal something of Christ's mystery. Christmas in the north is a midwinter feast, celebrated at nature's ebb-tide. However artificial the conditions of modern living, however out of touch people may be with the earth and its cycles of growth and decay, it makes for sanity and wholeness if we can still respond through our bodies to the elemental experiences from which our forbears learnt wisdom. Winter means darkness, cold, and apparent barrenness; or, more precisely, a sensory experience of certain contrasts: darkness and light, frozenness and thaw, sterility and fruitfulness.

The alternation of light and darkness is a primary experience, and has easily passed into being a primary symbol in human consciousness. Most children fear the dark, and probably our ancestors did too, with good reason. European peoples have certainly been very sensitive to the ebb and flow of light and darkness since prehistoric times. Midwinter

---

* The substance of this chapter is from a talk entitled 'The Winter Feast', first broadcast by the author on BBC Radio Three, Christmas Day 1981.

darkness must have been a vast, powerful, mysterious reality for generations with no electricity or gas and very little oil. The forests were much thicker and more extensive than today, and there were no lighted buildings or motorways to provide islands or strips of luminosity: only a huge engulfing darkness of which people were afraid. It was not only superstitious terror; the winter was a time to dread, when food would be short, some members of the tribe might die, and everyone would be cold and hungry.[2] The darkness must have profoundly affected people's lives and the way they perceived their world. The growth or shrinkage of daylight was therefore a matter of intense concern, and the bodies of primitive peoples were more responsive to these changes and to all nature's moods than are those of modern town-dwellers. The megalithic monuments which still stir our imagination at Avebury, Stonehenge and other places were often carefully sited with reference to sunrise and sunset. For all northern peoples the winter solstice was an important turning-point. Almost imperceptibly at first, the vast darkness was beginning to lose ground.

Further south, in the lands around the Mediterranean, the homes of ancient cultures, the sun came to symbolize all that people longed for: life, wholeness, immortality. In Egypt, hopes and beliefs in life after death were connected with Re or Ra, the sun-god. Each evening Re's boat disappeared in the west, he travelled through the underworld during the night and reappeared in the east next morning. In Greece, myths deified Helios. Roman peasants worshipped the sun, and by about the beginning of the Christian era sun-symbolism had won a place in the state religion of the Roman Empire. The feast of the Unconquered Sun, *Natalis Solis Invicti*, was kept at or near the winter solstice: at the time when he seemed to have been defeated the sun was beginning to roll back the darkness.

In the fourth century this Roman midwinter feast of the Unconquered Sun was captured by Christianity and reinterpreted. It became the feast of Christ's birth, the special Incarnation festival, 'Christmas'. This was a stroke of genius which was to influence the Christian mind and imagination

27

very powerfully in the centuries to come. Christ's birth was a dawning brightness from on high. People remembered Malachi's prophecy: 'For you who fear my name the sun of righteousness shall rise, with healing in his wings' (Mal. 4.2, NEB).

The biblical tradition helped this reinterpretation. Israel, the people of promise, had learnt the meaning of darkness and light in a certain historic night that marked their own birth as God's people, the night of their escape from Egypt. Through the darkness their God had gone before them, a pillar of fire. All through their history they were a people on the march, sometimes physically, always spiritually. God was always out ahead, faithful indeed, but surprising. They needed light to walk by, and looked to him:

> Your word is a lamp for my steps
> and a light for my path. . . .
> (Ps. 119 (118).105, Grail)

> The Lord is my light and my help;
> whom shall I fear?
> (Ps. 27 (26).1, Grail)

In the beginning, before God's creative act, there had been nothing, and this non-being was imagined by Israel as a chaotic darkness. Over the dark, formless void hovered the Spirit of God, and God's first work of creation was to call forth light; the account on the first page of Genesis is both poetic and practical, because of course he would have needed light to do the rest of the work:

> The earth was without form and void, and darkness was upon the face of the deep; and the Spirit of God was moving over the face of the waters. And God said, 'Let there be light'; and there was light. And God saw that the light was good; and God separated the light from the darkness.
> (Gen. 1.2-4)

The light is positive and blessed; darkness is pushed back, but left within its appointed limits. From that first page of Genesis until the end of the Book of Revelation, God's people travels towards a light that will roll back darkness for ever. The new Jerusalem is to be a brilliant place, for night will be abolished, and God himself will be the all-sufficient light for his saints:

> The city has no need of sun or moon to shine upon it, for the glory of God is its light, and its lamp is the Lamb. . . . And night shall be no more; they need no light of lamp or sun, for the Lord will be their light.
> (Rev. 21.23; 22.5)

From here it is a short step to St John's simple assertion, 'God is light, and in him is no darkness at all' (1 John 1.5).

Every saving intervention of God was like a dawn after the darkness of fear and affiction, and dawn was in a special way the moment when his saving help could be expected. A psalmist knew that Jerusalem could be confident, because

> God is within, it cannot be shaken;
> God will help it at the dawning of the day.
> (Ps. 46 (45).6, Grail)

At the time when an Assyrian invading force had deported peoples from Galilee, an oracle in the Book of Isaiah promised a merciful act of God which would reverse their fortunes:

> The people who walked in darkness has seen a great light;
> those who dwelt in a land of deep darkness,
> on them has light shone.[3]

All Israel's prayer for help, and for final salvation, was like a watch through the night, with eyes straining towards the place where dawn would break with the promise of God's coming:

> I wait for the Lord, my soul waits,
> and in his word I hope;
> my soul waits for the Lord
> more than watchmen for the morning,
> more than watchmen for the morning.
> (Ps. 130 (129). 5–6)

St John's Gospel gathers all these threads concerned with

light. Jesus is identified with the eternal creative Word of God; he is 'the true light that enlightens every man, coming into the world' (John 1.9). He is the new pillar of fire, and he summons men to follow him: 'I am the light of the world; he who follows me will not walk in darkness, but will have the light of life' (John 8.12). He gives the light of physical sight to the man born blind, who stands for all of us stranded in our native darkness, and in the same act gives him the light of faith to accept Jesus as the one who has been sent (cf. John 9). As John's Gospel moves towards the full revelation of Jesus's 'glory', we are aware of darkness closing in, threatening to choke the light. Jesus urgently warns the disciples:'The light is with you for a little while longer. Walk while you have the light, lest the darkness overtake you' (John 12.35). It seems as though he is half speaking to himself. Coming to his last supper he gathers his own in the brightness of the room where he will give them the uttermost proof of his love, but the powers of darkness are at work, and Judas goes out into the night.

The Synoptic Gospels speak of a darkness like a solar eclipse on the afternoon of the crucifixion. The week of the great struggle, the week of the new creation, ends with a Sabbath of rest, as Jesus lies in the tomb, but all the Gospels move towards the dawn of the first day of the new week. In the early light, the time of divine victory according to Israelite tradition, the greatest miracle of God's saving work is made known: Christ has been drawn from the darkness of death. His risen manhood is alight with the unquenchable glory of the Father. The light has shone in our darkness, and darkness has been unable to master it, though it has done its utmost.

Christianity arrived in the world of pagan culture with firm beliefs grounded in this Old Testament tradition and in history. The sun was no god but a creature of the true God. Helios was demythologized, but the very firmness and clarity of Christian belief made it possible to welcome the poetry and imaginative power inherent in the cult of sun, moon and stars. The sun-symbolism developed by the ancient world was taken over by the Christian Fathers.

Christ's passion was like a sunset. There was a striking parallel between the three days of the Easter mystery and the journey of the sun. On Friday Christ died, on Saturday his body rested in the grave but tradition said he visited the underworld for the 'harrowing of hell', and on Sunday – the 'Sun's day' – he rose again: it paralleled the sun's setting, its nocturnal journey under the earth and its new rising.

It was obvious that the solar symbolism fitted the Easter mystery. But the new Testament in several places speaks of Christ's resurrection as a birth: according to Paul he is the 'first-born from the dead' (Col. 1.18). It was therefore easy to extend the sun-symbolism to his birth as a child at Bethlehem. So the feast of the winter solstice was baptized, and became 'Christmas'.

As the midwinter sun-feast of Christmas spread northwards, it gathered to itself all the northern magic, stirring ancient memories in people for whom winter was both fierce and fascinating. There is an ambivalence about winter: even today volunteer teachers who work in village schools in the fishing ports of Greenland may find the children impossible to control when the first smell of winter is in the air, and these children are not the only people who are thrilled by it.[4] Scandinavians still honour the feast of St Lucy, the light-bringer saint, in December, with a deep sense of ancient observances made Christian. There is a special glory in a red winter sunset in England, when the sun looks different through the frosty air, and a piercing beauty about a mid-afternoon sunset when the black, gaunt skeletons of trees allow the red-gold to shine through them in a way they never could in their summer prosperity. The long nights are full of stars. Night too is ambivalent: it is an image of death and of the empire of nameless terrors, but it is also rest, peace and healing, the time when worlds are born. And without night we should never see the stars.

The northern darkness was all too real, however, and the missionaries spoke a language northern peoples could understand. Yes, they explained, the promised light of the world has indeed come, the Dayspring from on high, and has delivered us from the dominion of darkness. The people who walked in darkness have seen a great light; for us who dwell in the shadow of death light has shone. The yoke of our burden has been lifted. Some of the glory spilled round shepherds who were keeping their watch through the night. And certain wise men came from the East – from the *East*, the sunrise place, as the Greek of Matthew makes clear – but they had unsatisfied hearts, and put their trust in the leading of a star in their long search through the night. They too came to the real light:

> Out of the dark primeval night,
> as from the womb of time,
> and all alone,
> came Man.
> When did he first look up
> and find the stars his friends?
> For a thousand times three thousand years
> they did not fail,
> in their circling paths of light,
> to stand above the dark
> keeping their promise safe,
> until from beyond their unimaginable end
> the Word went forth.
> And Eastern Kings
> saw how their magic paled.
> And Glory stood above the cave-born child.[5]

The Christian East has tended to observe the Epiphany as the feast of the manifestation of Christ at his baptism in the Jordan. This was a prophetic sign of his descent into the dark waters of death and his rising as God's Son in power. It orients us towards 'Christ our Light' in his Easter, and to the celebration of baptism, which the early Church called 'Illumination'. But in the West the Magi, the wise men, have caught our imagination, and they dominate the feast of the Epiphany. In Matthew's Infancy Gospel they represent the Gentiles, come to do homage to the Saviour who is born King of the Jews. They recall to Matthew's readers the obscure prophecy of Balaam, another seer from the East, who predicted that

> A star shall come forth out of Jacob,
> and a sceptre shall rise out of Israel.[6]

The very simple shepherds, and the learned, experienced, disillusioned sages who had been through it all – to both was manifested the light that shone quietly in the darkness.[7]

As a contrapuntal theme, John the Baptist appears as an Advent saint, the Forerunner, not himself the light but only a lamp and a voice, preparing the way for the Lord's coming. He has given the formula for Christian asceticism: 'Christ must increase, I must decrease', and so he very properly celebrates his own feast at midsummer, just when daylight begins to diminish.

It may be questioned whether all this symbolism, so powerful for earlier generations, can still speak to us today. Most people in the developed countries are independent of natural light, since they can create 'daylight' at any moment in the twenty-four hours by touching a switch. Winter is less noticeable in well-lit, centrally heated buildings, except for the sharp rise in fuel bills. Nevertheless the modern world knows a darkness of mind and spirit that can match anything our Stone Age or Bronze Age ancestors feared. Technological brilliance alone cannot illumine the human spirit. Our society has lost its way in a darkness as real as that of the ancient world. People walk in the shadow of death today, in a mental and spiritual darkness which engulfs those who, without hope, lonely, empty and afraid, try to keep going in a life that seems to be without direction or meaning.

The light of Christ is in us and among us if we consent to let it be, and it is diffused by people who are prepared to be translucent, but only if we have allowed it to show us up first, and have faced the darkness in ourselves. Christian life and prayer are not an uninterrupted enjoyment of the light. Great mystical writers speak of painful 'nights' of sense and spirit, not an exciting adventure reserved for the few but the experience of anyone who follows Christ through the darkness to his Easter. Mercifully, the light shed by such a person is often visible to the rest of us, even when its bearer is conscious only of walking weakly in the dark.

Cold is an ugly, painful element in human experience. It is a threat to life. Birds and small animals may die in winter; so do many people living near the starvation line, and some old people living alone; there is a depth of suffering hidden under that clinical term, 'hypothermia'. For the rest of us cold may not be a threat in that sense, but it does lower our level of life, reducing us to misery, to preoccupation with our elemental needs, and to a marked reluctance to act in any imaginative, unselfish or constructive way. It sets us wondering how people managed in draughty medieval castles where the only fire was in the banqueting hall. Dante envisaged part of Upper Hell as cold, and one feels he had a point.[8]

However unpleasant, this is a very basic human experience, one which we share with millions in the past and the present. We also share in some way in the general frozenness, sterility and apparent death of nature. Yet we know that winter is necessary, precisely for the rebirth of nature which delights us every spring. The earth sleeps, holding its seeds in trust, waiting. The trees sleep, preparing for the great work of spring and summer, for flowering and fruit-bearing. In countries where it is always warm the climate can force roses into bloom all the year round, but they are not as good as the roses of the cold countries, because they miss their winter sleep.

Frost is clean, and has its own beauty. Even the biblical writers, living generally in warmer regions, marvelled at frost and thaw:

> He spreads frost on the earth like salt,
> and icicles form like pointed stakes.
> A cold blast from the north,
> and ice grows hard on the water,
> settling on every pool,
> as though the water were putting on a breastplate.
> (Sirach (Ecclus.) 43.19–20, NEB)

But then

> He sends forth his word and it melts them:
> at the breath of his mouth the waters flow.
> (Ps. 147.18, Grail)

Part of the northern magic in Sigrid Undset's great novel of fourteenth-century Norway is the description of a desperately hard and long winter, when food is running short and it seems the thaw will never come. The days have lengthened, but the cold goes on and on. Then at last:

> Far on in the night Kristin was wakened in the dark by her father's touch on her shoulder.
>
> 'Get up,' he said softly. 'Do you hear—?'
>
> She heard the singing of the wind round the house-corners – the deep, full note of the south wind, heavy with wetness. Streams were pouring from the roof; there was the whisper of rain falling on soft, melting snow. . . . They stood together looking out into the twilight of the May night. Warm wind and rain smote against them; the heavens were a welter of tangled drifting rain-clouds, the woods roared, the wind whistled between the houses, and from far up in the fells they heard the dull boom of snow-masses falling.[9]

Whether in winter or in the desert, water and wind and word are a life-bearing triad. Water heals the waste land.

The paralysis of nature in winter is a kind of northern equivalent of the biblical desert, the condition of no life, no growth, no promise. The difference is that we know winter will pass. The desert is a 'land unsown', with no opening towards the future. Israel had known it, the unforgettable desert of their birth:

> You shall remember all the way which the Lord your God has led you these forty years in the wilderness, that he might humble you, testing you to know what was in your heart, whether you would keep his commandments, or not. And he humbled you, and let you hunger and fed you with manna. . . .[10]

They failed the test, and what was in their hearts was sin: murmuring, lack of trust, despair, turning in on themselves, rejection of the call to love, betrayal of the covenant and refusal to see the desert as the place for knowing the Lord

35

and the way to the land of promise. Yet this wilderness where they confronted their sin and unfaith was also the place where they knew the faithfulness of God. He led them, provided for them, gave them bread from heaven and water from the rock, and finally brought their children to the 'exceedingly good land'. Israel 'looked steadfastly towards the wilderness' (Exod. 16.10) and there, in that unlikely place, they saw the glory of God.

Later Israel looked back at that exodus experience; the generation that went into exile in Babylon in the sixth century BC had particular reason to remember it, because their own situation forced them to a poignant reliving of it. Yet they were in worse case. The wilderness wandering of the exodus had been part of the high adventure of Israel's beginnings, the time of covenant-making and first love, and even the sin which had been remembered with such honesty could be regarded by a later, sadder and wiser generation as the sin of childhood. The promises had been new and unrealized then, and they had had everything to learn. There were no such excuses now. After all Yahweh had done for them, after all their experiences of his love and fidelity, they had betrayed him and broken the covenant. He had given them the land of promise, and they had lost it again through their sins. The stretch of desert between them and the desolate land of Judah was an image of the desert in their hearts.

This is the kind of desert with which we too are familiar. The desert in our lives is the place where in our poverty, our sin and our need we come to know the Lord. For us too it is the place of the essential confrontations, where the irrelevancies are stripped away and the elemental things become all-important, where the truth in our hearts is revealed.

In prayer we are led into this desert, and there, away from the masks and camouflages, we have to stand in the truth. Prayer is very humbling, for you have nothing to shield you from the truth as you stand there before God day after day in your naked poverty. But to flee from this humbling experience is useless; we have to live with our own darkness, failure, temptation, confusion and weakness, because it is the only way in which these areas in us can be opened up to the Lord of the wilderness. We have to look steadfastly towards the wilderness of our own being, and it may be that there, in that unlikely place, we shall see the glory of the Lord.

Our desert is any situation of stripping, of hopelessness, of chaos; it is the place of sterility and loneliness, and there is nothing as sterile and lonely as sin. Of these desert areas also he is Lord. They can be opened up to him and become the place of new life. Sin and suffering often seem inextricably mixed in this desert experience, because when the pressure is on us and we are afraid, tempted and in pain, we know the humbling truth of our selfishness and betrayals. We never feel we have come through creditably. In mental suffering and depression it may be nearly impossible for us to know what is our own fault and what is a desert time that we have to endure, but fortunately it is not we who have to sort that out. The desert is only the real desert when it is too big for you, when you cannot see it as spiritually significant, when you do not know your way and have no reliance except God.

Our desert is any place where we confront God. It is not a change of scene, nor a place to run from our failures, nor a heroic adventure that does something for our ego. Our desert experience may be tedium, weariness, disappointment, loneliness, personal emptiness, emotional confusion, the feeling that we have nothing to give, the conviction that we constantly fail God in prayer. You just have to keep on keeping on in prayer, and you are not aware of 'progress', because there seems to be nothing by which it could be measured. There are no paths in the desert except the ones you make by walking on them.

It is the place of truth, but also of tenderness; the place of loneliness but also of God's closeness and care. The journey is precarious, but he is faithful, even though our own fidelity is shaky. In the place of hunger and poverty of spirit we are fed by the word of God, as Jesus himself was in the desert. Part of our poverty may be that we are not even aware of longing for God, only aware of the suffocating burden of our own sinfulness, of the slum within. But the desert is the place of confrontation not just with our sins, but with the power of God's redemption. You come to see it as the place where there can be springing water, manna to keep you going, the strength you never knew you had, the surprise of the quail that plops down at your feet, a tenderness that cares for you and a knowing of the Lord. These things are not the promised land, but they are tokens of love and may be sacraments of glory. Your life, your prayer, can be the wilderness to which you must look steadfastly if you would see the glory of God.

To the disoriented and desolate generation of the exile, pondering these things in the bleak sterility of a situation without hope, with no opening towards the future, Second Isaiah spoke the Lord's message of unparalleled tenderness:

> Behold, the Lord God comes with might,
> and his arm rules for him. . . .
> He will feed his flock like a shepherd,
> he will gather the lambs in his arms,
> he will carry them in his bosom,
> and gently lead those that are with young.
> (Isa. 41.10-11)

> For a brief moment I forsook you,
> but with great compassion I will gather you.
> In overflowing wrath for a moment I hid my face from you,
> but with everlasting love I will have compassion on you,
> says the Lord, your Redeemer.
> (Isa. 54.7-8)

The exodus from Egypt long ago is remembered, but only as a pledge of the still greater wonders that God's saving love has in store for them now. Long ago they made their way to the promised land by a long desert trek, but now the desert which stretches between the exiles and home will blossom and be transformed:

> I will open rivers on the bare heights,
> and fountains in the midst of the valleys;
> I will make the wilderness a pool of water,
> and the dry land springs of water.

I will put in the wilderness the cedar,
the acacia, the myrtle and the olive;
I will set in the desert the cypress,
the plane and the pine together;
that men may see and know. . .
that the hand of the Lord has done this.
(Isa. 41.18-20)

For I will pour water on the thirsty land,
and streams on the dry ground;
I will pour my Spirit upon your descendants,
and my blessing on your offspring.
They shall spring up like grass amid waters,
like willows by flowing streams.
(Isa. 44.3-4)

The moments of helpless need are the blessed times. These displaced persons were called, as we also are called, to heroic hope in God's power, promise and creative love. They hated their suffering, they could make no sense of it, they were bankrupt of human and spiritual resources. The Lord summoned them to trust him, to look for his new mercies. The wonders of old would seem almost negligible:

Remember not the former things,
nor consider the things of old.
Behold, I am doing a new thing.
(Isa. 43.18-19)

In the winters of our despair and sterility, in our personal desert or the hopeless situation of our nation or family or community, the Lord of the wilderness summons us to absolute faith in his new deed.

They had to wait for it, and so do we. Advent is the consecration of waiting in our lives. Human life is full of waiting: people wait for trains, buses and planes; they stand in queues at shops; they sit nervously in dentists' waiting-rooms; they wait in anguish for news of a lost loved one. They wait for the slow process of healing to take its time; they wait for the birth of a child. Waiting can be very different in these different situations, according to our attitude. In an age of 'instant' products any delay can be viewed as purely negative, for 'time is money'. Yet some things cannot be skimped or hurried; we have to let them take the time they need. You can't make the grass grow by pulling it, as the proverb wisely warns. In Chapter 2 we thought of faith as a breakthrough, the leap towards the invitation of the Lover. But it is not like that all the time. In between those obviously creative moments, faith can demand long, patient waiting, when nothing seems to be happening, and this is just as necessary to growth. We sometimes have to go on doing the small, ordinary things while we wait for God, as Mary did while she waited for the birth of Jesus; we have to wait for his moment, and wait for his work to ripen in ourselves. It may sometimes be more fruitful in the end if we live with a lingering question, and grow slowly towards wisdom, than if we find a quick answer partly dictated by our own desires. The waiting changes us, schools us, teaches us to know God:

> The Lord waits to be gracious to you. . . .
> Blessed are all those who wait for him.
> (Isa. 30.18)

In the lives of those who believe and pray, there are bleak winters of the spirit. We seem to go along well for a while in prayer and relationships and life generally, but from time to time we disintegrate. It is very painful. You may suspect that this will prove to be a creative disintegration, that God is re-creating you, putting you together in the likeness of his Son at a new and deeper level. Certainly this does happen: growth is not easy; there is a probably distressing period for the caterpillar on the way to butterflyhood. We are all participants in this experience from time to time, and a chrysalis needs sympathetic understanding, so we should be gentle and patient with ourselves, as with others. Nevertheless, they are hard to live through, these winters of the spirit. When you know yourself to be sterile, helpless, unable to deal creatively with your situation or change your own heart, you know your need for a Saviour, and you know what

Advent is. God brings us to these winters, these dreary times of deadness and emptiness of spirit, as truly as he brings winter after autumn, as a necessary step towards next spring. But while we are in them they feel like a real absence of God, or our absence from him:

> How like a winter hath my absence been
> From thee, the pleasure of the fleeting year!
> What freezings have I felt, what dark days seen!
> What old December's bareness everywhere![11]

Or, as Shakespeare has it even more poignantly in another sonnet:

> Yet seemed it winter still, and you away.[12]

Looking back, you know that these times brought you closer to the Lord of the winter, that it was necessary for you to go through them. In the winters of your prayer, when there seems to be nothing but darkness and a situation of general frozenness, hold on, wait for God. He will come.

Meanwhile, it is not all dead loss, any more than the winter of the fields is wasted. It is a creative time, even if we do not perceive it so. Our strength can sometimes be a greater obstacle to God's work than our weakness. The key moments in the history of salvation, the vital moments remembered in the Christian creeds, were moments not of action but of freely accepted passivity: Mary's consent to the Word becoming flesh, Jesus's crucifixion and his being raised from the dead. When people are making demands on you and you feel drained and empty; when you have to speak and you have not had the time you wanted to prepare; when God calls you to a task for which you know yourself inadequate; when you feel humiliated and foolish because some undertaking in which you did your honest best has turned out disastrously – then, it may be, to your astonishment, someone will tell you that you helped most, did your most fruitful work. When our ego is humbled and not obstructing, God's creative Spirit can often have freer play. Like the bare trees, it may be that we allow the glory to shine through at these times more purely than in our summer prosperity.

41

God seems to like this pattern. He whittled down Gideon's strong army to a paltry three hundred, the better to fight the Midianites on Israel's behalf (cf. Judg. 6). He frequently chose a younger brother in preference to an elder: Abel rather than Cain, Isaac before Ishmael, Jacob before Esau, Ephraim before Manasseh, David who was the youngest of his brothers. He chooses the weak things of this world to confound the strong. One of the clearest instances is a theme beloved of the Old Testament and oriented to the New, the story of barren women who through God's promise and their responsive faith bore the children of destiny.

The crucial promise to Abraham pointed to the birth of an heir, when he and his wife were too old for it to seem possible. Abraham believed and waited, and at last the child was born, fruit of the wedding between Abraham's long faith and the ever-young creative power of God. Rebekah was barren until Isaac prayed, and then she bore twin sons. Through Jacob the promise was handed on, but although he was well provided with offspring, his favourite wife Rachel was barren at first. Eventually she bore Joseph, who was to save his people in the famine years. As Israel at the time of the exodus wandered in a barren wilderness, so the patriarchs before them had barren wives; there is a parallel between the absent growth in the 'land unsown' and the missing heir of Abraham. In neither case does there seem to be any hope for the future.

With Hannah, at first barren and humiliated, then, after her prayer, the joyful mother of Samuel, the theme is explicitly related to the tradition of Yahweh's poor:

> My heart exults in the Lord;
> my strength is exalted in the Lord.
> My mouth derides my enemies,
> because I rejoice in thy salvation. . . .
> The bows of the mighty are broken,
> but the feeble gird on strength.
> Those who were full have hired themselves out for bread,
> but those who were hungry have ceased to hunger.
> The barren has borne seven,
> but she who has many children is forlorn. . . .

> The Lord makes poor and makes rich;
> he brings low, he also exalts.
> He raises up the poor from the dust;
> he lifts the needy from the ash heap,
> to make them sit with princes
> and inherit a seat of honour.[13]

Perhaps it was the *'anawim*, some centuries after Hannah's day, who put into her mouth this exultant song which sounds like a prelude to the Magnificat. She stood out as a symbol of the vindication of the poor, because barrenness was a particularly sharp, even agonizing, form of personal poverty. The Lord's 'blessing' was commonly held to result in prosperity of every kind for those who received it: the power to succeed, victory over one's enemies, fertility in fields and flocks, a long life and numerous descendants. Throughout most of the Old Testament period hope in a future life was undeveloped and shadowy, so to prolong one's life in that of one's children and grandchildren was the primary way to ensure survival. Childlessness was a disaster and, for a woman especially, a disgrace.

The experience of barrenness was communal as well as personal, and linked with the violation of the covenant. Jerusalem was a great archetypal symbol in the minds of the people of promise: Jerusalem, the bride of Yahweh, bound to him in the marriage bond of the covenant, cherished and protected by his faithful love, was destined to bear him many children. Yet the unfaithful city was ravaged at the time of the Babylonian invasion, stripped of her strength and her children and left desolate:

> What can I say for you, to what compare you,
> O daughter of Jerusalem?
> What can I liken to you, that I may comfort you,
> O virgin daughter of Zion?
> For vast as the sea is your ruin;
> who can restore you?
> (Lam. 2.13)

The appellation, 'virgin daughter of Zion', is no title of

honour; rather it evokes her lonely, forlorn condition and the general hopelessness of her state. She is barren.

Yet the mercy and power of God are greater than her sin, and in her reconciliation with him she will know a fruitfulness beyond all imagining. It will be sheer gift:

> Sing, O barren one, who did not bear;
> break forth into singing and cry aloud,
> you who have not been in travail!
> For the children of the desolate one will be more
> than the children of her that is married, says the Lord.
> Enlarge the place of your tent . . .
> hold not back, lengthen your cords
> and strengthen your stakes.
> For you will spread abroad to the right and to the left,
> and your descendants will possess the nations
> and will people the desolate cities.
> (Isa. 54.1–3)

The transformation of another case of hopeless barrenness is recalled:

> Look to Abraham your father
> and to Sarah who bore you;
> for he was but one when I called him,
> and I blessed him and made him many.
> (Isa. 51.2)

Remembering these things, Luke opens his Gospel with a picture of a little group of *'anawim*, people of faith and prayer, waiting in poverty of spirit for the comforting of Israel. Zechariah and Elizabeth are elderly and childless; the allusion is not far to seek. By the promise and ever-young power of God the forerunner of salvation is conceived, and the angel points to this unlooked-for conception of John as a sign for Mary: 'This is the sixth month with her who was called barren, for with God nothing will be impossible' (Luke 1.36–7). But John, like all the other children of promise, is only a sign of the utter gratuitousness of the self-gift of God.

Mary's virginity at the time of the Annunciation is poverty and emptiness, but an emptiness that is waiting and a poverty that is unimpeded openness to God. The Lover of Israel, the Lover of mankind, asks and waits. The humility of God is devastating, and he will not force consent; he asks for the body he needs, of the flesh and blood of Israel. Mary consents, and the last barrier is down. Salvation is pure gift. Where human resources, human potency, human self-sufficiency are lacking, but there is humble, hopeful faith, Love gives itself finally and utterly.

The childbearing of the barren women has pointed to this:

> Love and truth in him shall flower,
> from his strength their vigour take.
> Branches that are bare shall blossom;
> joy that slept begins to wake.[14]

The long winter is over, and the frost has broken up the earth for its task. God speaks his creative word:

> As the rain and the snow come down from heaven,
> and return not thither but water the earth,
> making it bring forth and sprout,
> giving seed to the sower and bread to the eater,
> so shall my word be that goes forth from my mouth;
> it shall not return to me empty,
> but it shall accomplish that which I purpose.
> (Isa. 55.10–11)

The Word made flesh is Son of God and Son of Mary. Salvation is wholly from above, the gift of heaven, yet it truly springs from our human soil. Second Isaiah heralded it in a verse which liturgical tradition has made into a theme-song for Advent:

> Rain righteousness, you heavens,
> let the skies above pour down;
> let the earth open to receive it,
> that it may bear the fruit of salvation.
> (Isa. 45.8, NEB)

Into the weary old creation the new thing has broken. The old creation was a first sketch of the new, a genuine ikon, and there is bodily connection between them; nevertheless

45

the new is more, infinitely more, than the old promised, and Mary's childbearing in virginity is a sign of this 'more'. Her womb was a 'void', like the lifeless void over which the Creator Spirit hovered at the world's beginning. The Spirit overshadows Mary, and God fills the void with the surprise of creation, with the child who is his Son. Jesus is a man within history, fully rooted in all that humanity means, enmeshed with us in the human genetic web and heir with us to the huge weight of experiences that relate us to all life, to that first breakthrough when life came to be. Yet he is virgin-born, as a sign that he is pure gift from above.

It is very difficult for us to grasp how these things can both be true at once. In practice it is only from the standpoint of Christ's resurrection that we can begin to understand the new creation which is inaugurated at his birth.[15] Our perspective is that of redeemed sinners. There is a darkness, a desert, a sterility of finitude; there is also a darkness, a desert, a sterility of sin. We cannot completely separate them in our sin-conditioned experience. For us, the new creation is born of forgiveness, and so our only models are paschal. The risen body of Jesus, and his whole risen manhood, are the same body and the same manhood that grew and worked, suffered and rejoiced, in all the experiences of earthly life, yet he is transfigured, new-born, in his rising from the dead. Again, a person born anew in grace is fully himself, with all his unique identity and characteristics, but he is a new creation. When God re-creates, he neither abolishes the old creation to begin all over again, nor merely tidies up the old by removing its blemishes. The new creation is something greater still. God 'throws' the elements anew. There is continuity, but a gift of a wholly different order.

Christ's birth of Mary is the inbreaking of this new creation. Fully one with us, he is yet new-born, as we shall all be, 'not of the will of the flesh nor of the will of man, but of God' (John 1.13). His human birth is the real, earthly, physical beginning of the redemptive process which will give us new birth as children of God, through his new birth from the dead.

4 Spring and New Birth

Spring has come again. Earth's a-bubble
with all those poems she knows by heart, –
oh, so many . . . . With prize for the trouble
of such long learning, her holidays start.

Stern was her teacher, he'd overtask her
from time to time; but we liked the snows
in the old man's beard; and now we can ask her
what green, what blue are: she knows, she knows.

Eager to catch you, Earth, happy creature,
play with the children now outpouring!
Conqueringly foremost the happiest springs.

All she has ever been taught by her teacher,
all that's imprinted in roots and soaring
difficult stems, – she sings, she sings![1]

Jesus is the thrice-born. Christian tradition honours his human birth at Bethlehem as a visible event between two invisible births: his eternal birth as Son of the Father in the splendours of the Trinity, and his birth by grace in the life of every human being who accepts him. All three of these births are real, but not all are historical. His trinitarian birth as the Father's Word is outside history, in the eternal Now of God's life. His human birth of Mary, from the stock of Israel, is an event in historical time, more or less datable. His hidden birth in people's lives takes place again and again, and will continue through all the time of human history.

Advent and Christmas are concerned with all three of these births, and so will this chapter be, but it is not possible to separate them and deal with each in turn. They are intertwined in mystery beyond mystery, depth beyond depth. The eternal, divine birth of the Son is the foundation

47

of all else. The coming to be of the whole created universe is an echo of that primordial utterance, as John declares:

> In the beginning was the Word, and the Word was with God, and the Word was God. He was in the beginning with God; all things were made through him, and without him was not anything made.
> (John 1.1–3)

The Father's being, identity and joy are to pour himself out unreservedly in his self-gift to his Son. The Son's being and delight are to have nothing as of himself but all as received in the gift of love, and to breathe his answering love to the Father. The New Testament speaks of the Son as the radiant splendour of the Father's glory; the Creed calls him 'God from God, Light from Light, true God from true God'. Early Christian writers speak of the Source and the Spring. These are images; as long as we remember that the reality behind them is infinitely personal they may help, but language breaks under the strain. The eternal begetting of the Son who is the Father's glory is beyond our understanding and imagination, because it is the innermost mystery of God.

Yet we can hear and speak, even of God, even of that primal birth, because God has made us in his image, as creatures who communicate, and our clumsy efforts to understand and love are an echo of his Word. Every movement of self-surrendering love in human relationships, every response of beloved to lover, every real personal communication and meeting of minds, is a shadow of that glory. Every utterance of passionate beauty proclaims it. All that we know of the dignity and joy of parenthood on earth points towards it. Life and love in our experience are flow and reflow, giving and receiving; the more we give, the more we receive and the more there is to give, and this is because we are a little like God. His life is not solitude, self-sufficiency or a frozen, static perfection. He is eternal exchange, infinite unselfishness. Love is never cornered, pinned down, halted in its flow, because it never finds a self to trap it and appropriate it. The three Persons are a dance of utter delight: they exist for one another.

The Christian Fathers pondered the question: given that God willed to become incarnate within his own creation, could any of the three Persons, Father, Son or Spirit, have been made man? Need it have been the Son? And they answer, There is supreme harmony in the incarnation of the Son. He is the Word in whom God created all things, and the redemption he wrought is a new creation. He, in his eternal reality, is the Son of the Father, and the purpose of his coming is to extend to us a share in God's life through our adoption as children of God within his sonship:

> To all who received him, who believed in his name, he gave power to become children of God; who were born, not of blood nor of the will of the flesh nor of the will of man but of God. And the Word became flesh. . . .[2]

'The Word became flesh.' Were our minds not blunted by familiarity we should be shocked by that statement. Even before the revelation of God's trinitarian life, before men knew that the Word was a Person, the 'word' of Yahweh in the Old Testament stood for what was strong and abiding. But 'flesh' meant weakness and transience. Second Isaiah put them side by side to point the contrast:

> All flesh is grass,
> and all its beauty is like the flower of the field.
> The grass withers, the flower fades,
> when the breath of the Lord blows upon it. . . .
> The grass withers, the flower fades;
> but the word of our God will stand for ever.
> (Isa. 40.6–8)

Yet the eternal Word was born flesh of our flesh, so that we, who could not grasp with our minds what was from the beginning, might see with our eyes and touch with our hands, and know his glory within our human experience. He has shared everything that is ours, in order to lift us into everything that is his. He is here, of the flesh of Mary, the flesh of the human family. 'Our Father who art in heaven' and our brother who art on earth, of one stock with us in the shared nature, Sanctifier and sanctified.

49

He was localized in time and space, and all the concrete earthiness of Israel's hope was vindicated. Bethlehem had been David's birthplace, and since the eighth century BC Micah's prophecy had linked it to the messianic hope:

> You, O Bethlehem, Ephrathah,
> who are little to be among the clans of Judah,
> from you shall come forth for me
> one who is to be ruler in Israel,
> whose origin is from of old,
> from ancient days.
> (Mic. 5.2)

The Davidic Messiah, the 'Anointed One' for whom Israel waited, was to be God's 'son' in an adopted sense. Great promises had been made in the Lord's name to every trembling boy at his coronation, until the monarchy foundered:

> The Lord said to me: 'You are my Son.
> It is I who have begotten you this day.
> Ask and I shall bequeath you the nations,
> put the ends of the earth in your possession.'
> (Ps. 2.7–8, Grail)

> He will say to me: 'You are my father,
> my God, the rock who saves me.'
> And I will make him my first-born. . . .
> (Ps. 89 (88).27–8, Grail)

> A prince from the day of your birth
> on the holy mountains;
> from the womb before the daybreak I begot you. . . .[3]

Hyperbolic and figurative these oracles had been, Yahwistic faith speaking with poetic licence. Then one night, in some obscure spot in Bethlehem, they were figurative no longer, except for falling far short of the reality. The birth probably made very little stir, and yet,

> O little town of Bethlehem,
>   How still we see thee lie!
> Above thy deep and dreamless sleep
>   The silent stars go by.

Yet in thy dark streets shineth
    The everlasting Light;
The hopes and fears of all the years
    Are met in thee to-night.[4]

The eternal Son who is 'the effulgence of God's splendour and the stamp of God's very being' (Heb. 1.3, NEB) was there as a baby: human, helpless and poor. Over this moment of piercing beauty artists, carol-singers and crib-makers have exulted down the centuries. Ephrem, the Syrian poet and deacon of the fourth century, was one of the earliest of many:

Blessed be that child, who gladdened Bethlehem today,
blessed be the babe, who made manhood young again. . . .
Glory to the Silence, who spoke by his Voice. . . .
Glory to that hidden One, whose Son was made
    manifest. . . .
Glory to that great One, whose Son descended and was
    small. . . .
By power from him
Mary was able to bear in her embrace him that bears up all
    things.
From the great storehouse of all creatures
Mary gave him all. . . .
She gave him milk from himself that prepared it,
she gave him food from himself that made it.
Her hands bore him in that he had lightened his strength,
her arm embraced him, in that he had made himself
    small. . . .
She wove for him and clothed him because he had put off
    his glory,
she measured him and wove for him, since he had made
    himself little. . . .
How mighty art thou, O child!
Thy judgement is mighty, and thy love is sweet. . . .
Thy Father is in heaven, thy mother on earth;
who shall declare thee?
If a man should seek after thy nature,
it is hidden in the mighty bosom of the godhead,
if a man seek after thy visible body,
it is laid in the little bosom of Mary.
The mind wanders between thy generations. . . .[5]

Part of the poignancy of the scene is that it is unrepeatable. History is like that; thousands of years converged upon that moment, and the little group at Bethlehem will never be found together again. They cannot even have stayed together for long then. The nativity scenes catch them poised in one historic moment, with all the poetry of the particular. It will not come again in history, but it is not lost, for all that. In God no beauty, no truth, no moment of glory can ever be lost. The uncreated beauty that spilled itself into history that night is waiting for us.

Meanwhile, there was life to be lived. The earthly trinity at Bethlehem were at the beginning of a journey. After forty days Luke shows Mary, the new Ark of the Covenant and cradle of the glory, carrying the child to the temple, from which Yahweh's glory departed at the time of the Babylonian conquest. There she meets Simeon, the old man who stands for the exhausted old covenant, and he recognizes the glory:

> This day, Master, thou givest thy servant his discharge
>   in peace;
> now thy promise is fulfilled.
> For I have seen with my own eyes
> the deliverance which thou hast made ready
> in full view of all the nations:
> a light that will be a revelation to the Gentiles
> and glory to thy people Israel.[6]

He is of the *'anawim*, and his old eyes have seen it. The old man holding the young child is an archetypal symbol. Not only is the time of preparation fulfilled; the Jewish way of life in Jerusalem will not endure much longer. Simeon represents its last years, as Eliot finely evokes him:

> Lord, the Roman hyacinths are blooming in bowls and
> The winter sun creeps by the snow hills;
> The stubborn season has made stand.
> My life is light, waiting for the death wind,
> Like a feather on the back of my hand.
> Dust in sunlight and memory in corners
> Wait for the wind that chills towards the dead land. . . .

Before the time of cords and scourges and lamentation
Grant us thy peace.
Before the stations of the mountain of desolation,
Before the certain hour of maternal sorrow,
Now at this birth season of decease,
Let the Infant, the still unspeaking and unspoken Word,
Grant Israel's consolation
To one who has eighty years and no tomorrow.[7]

Mary is young and has many tomorrows. She is spring after the old man's winter; she is the Israel who will make the transition, the breakthrough, the passionate passover in Christ to God's future. She stands for Israel even as Simeon foretells the sword-thrust of sorrow for her people that will tear her heart, and the agony of division around her child, who is to be the sign of contradiction. She does not understand, either at this moment or at many another to come, but she ponders the word in her heart.

They lived together, mother and child and legal father, in all the closeness and love demanded by their own hearts and their relationship. We have no way of knowing how much of the mystery surfaced in the minds of all three of them as they pondered the prophecies and prayers of their people, how much they were able, or dared, to articulate. After the time of his babyhood only one hint is given of anything strange. Luke's Infancy Gospel concludes with the episode of Jesus at twelve years old being lost in Jerusalem. The story can be read, and makes perfect sense, at a purely human level, as a stage in his development towards manhood and adult membership of the community of Israel, but it is also like a first sketch of Easter. Luke mentions for the first time a journey from Galilee to Jerusalem, foreshadowing another great journey to Jerusalem which Jesus will make in Luke's account of his ministry.[8] It culminates in the feast of passover, as his later journey will lead him to his own passover. He is lost for a symbolic period of three days. Mary and Joseph suffer and agonize and search for him, just as later the women who went with him to Calvary will mourn and seek him. On finding him Mary says, 'Your father and I

53

have been looking for you anxiously', and he asks her, 'How is it that you sought me?', as later in the garden he will ask another woman, 'For whom are you searching?' (John 20.15). He takes up Mary's phrase, 'your father', but uses it in a different sense: 'Did you not know that I must be in *my Father's* house?' He has acted out in prophetic sign his paschal return to his Father. Yet the incident has all the psychological naturalness of an adolescent's impulse to claim his freedom, and even of a mistake on the part of a boy who has just broken through to a new and dizzying realization that God is his Father, and has drawn the wrong conclusion as to what action is appropriate. There is always a natural, human correlate to a prophetic action or the 'fulfilment of a prophecy'. People do not stage things self-consciously; they act as, at the highest of their understanding and responsiveness to God, they see to be required of them.

Jesus was fully human, not only in body but also in mind and spirit, and to be human is not a static condition but a process of growth. The birth we celebrate at Christmas was the gateway to an open-ended adventure, a life-project. He was confronted in his dawning understanding with the task confronting us all: to become maturely human through discovery, growth, interaction with other people, and risk. He was no Peter Pan, clinging to the securities of childhood; indeed, the birth stories themselves suggest otherwise. Peter Pan would have gathered all the children round him and gone off on a glorious picnic. Jesus escapes as the Innocents are massacred. He who is to be the Saviour of his people is snatched from the hatred of a wicked king, like Moses long ago.[9]

The child motif in Scripture, myths, literature and life is ambivalent. Childhood may be beautiful and idyllic, but only when chronologically appropriate. The Peter Pan syndrome is a clinging to the world of childhood and a refusal to face the challenge of new birth to a fuller life; it is sinister and in the end death-dealing, because there can be no genuine giving or unselfish love, nor truthful acceptance of reality.[10] The other aspect of the child motif is Jung's archetype of the

Miraculous Child, symbol of new life and promise, the vision of a new beginning, the possibility of growth, maturity and the new attempt.[11]

This is the Christmas child. His passage through the 'narrow door to light' led to a life in which he would be reborn many times. He began 'the intolerable wrestle with words and meanings'. He began to listen, from within his human condition and with the unfolding resources of his human mind, to the Father's word of love. Within our race, amid the opaqueness of the sin-situation, there was someone saying 'Abba' with a human voice, mind and heart, someone struggling to meet the love that called to him in prayer, in people and in every experience. The human longing in him met the divine longing, God's longing to give himself to humankind. Because the two longings met in the heart of Jesus, and because obedience to that love shaped the whole course of his life and death, the two longings have leaped to meet one another in innumerable other human lives.

Jesus took on the weight of human history, and with it the conditioning we all inherit from forgotten ancestors and from the play of unknown forces that shaped their attitudes and choices. He was not 'man' in some impersonal sense, but *a man*, with all that for us is a *sine qua non* of human existence, 'the nexus of biological, historical and social relationships with our fellow-men and with the universe as a whole'.[12] The Christian Fathers delighted to repeat, 'What has not been assumed [by the incarnate Son] has not been healed'. There is nothing in our human experience that he has not been through from the inside; the idea of Jesus travelling through life with some kind of divine immunization against failure, ignorance, passion and laughter is intolerable. The only experience he did not share was sin, and that was no disadvantage, since it makes us less human; in any case he felt the full impact of evil to a degree of intensity the rest of us can scarcely conceive. All the tedium, weariness, pain, joy and exhilaration, all the effort to understand and grow, all the love given and received that make life human, he knew. The recalcitrant situations, the ambiguities, the gaps between what should be and what is, he accepted and lived from the inside, making of the whole dislocated human condition the place of response to that Love which stood behind the barrier, asking.

Jesus accepted limitations and used them creatively. Every creator works within limitations; to work with them rather than fighting them is part of the challenge: the form of the symphony, the grain of the wood, the strict confines of the sonnet, the painful pruning of the young tree. Art feeds on sacrifice, and small is beautiful. The incarnation is God's supreme, most glorious work of art, and he accepts the limitations of operating within a finite nature.[13] This is a divine decision, but in due course it involved human decisions too. Jesus the man, with all the sensitivity of a young, vitally intelligent, exceedingly able and passionately loving human being, lived within limitations: the cultural narrowness of an upcountry Galilean village, the lack of formal education, scarcely any travel outside his own country, the obtuse minds of disciples with whom he longed to share the understanding he was struggling to articulate to himself, and the crowds who pressed upon him, nearly stifled him, ate up all his time and cut across his plans. All this must have meant genuine, lifelong human suffering, but it was creatively accepted and used as the raw material of obedient love. His Father, to whom he escaped at times for long stretches of prayer, was immensity and space to breathe, to breathe the Spirit of their mutual love through his human prayer. He must have needed the space, the silence, the call to stretch beyond the narrowness of day-to-day ministry, but for all that, it was within the narrow confines that he knew the Father and listened to his word. By creatively accepting the limitations he invested them with Easter significance, and thereby empowered us to do the same.

Nearly everyone who prays and tries to love God is aware of cramping situations, from being handicapped to being financially squeezed. Jesus too was handicapped in a sense, but he lived with it and used it. This is not to contradict what was said earlier about the Peter Pan syndrome. There is a world of difference between *wanting* the confining status, conditions or rituals of childhood because they represent security, and the humble acceptance of inevitable limitations as the way of obedience. The former is part of a back-to-the-womb urge, the latter part of the central Easter experience.

Jesus's ministry and his understanding of his vocation were directed to releasing human beings from all that constrained and cramped them in their response to love. Early in the public life Luke shows him in the synagogue at Nazareth claiming the Isaian passage about the prophet to the poor as a reference to himself:

> He opened the book and found the place where it was written,
> 'The Spirit of the Lord is upon me,
> because he has anointed me to preach the good news to the poor.
> He has sent me to proclaim release to the captives
> and recovering of sight to the blind,
> to set at liberty those who are oppressed. . . .'
> And he began to say to them, 'Today this scripture has been fulfilled in your hearing.'[14]

These forms of captivity were seen as symptoms of the grip of evil on mankind, and his mission was to break that grip and set people free. But he did it by allowing evil to mobilize a total onslaught on himself, and receiving it with love. As he had accepted the constrictions of his life for no other reason but love, and had been reborn many times through those narrow passages, so he came to accept the ultimate constrictions of death. He went through 'the time of cords and scourges', the final diminishment and the narrow passage of death for no other reason but love, and so in the most crushing physical unfreedom he was free. Evil had lost its power to constrain love, and the breakthrough to the new birth of his resurrection was the triumph of a love free to celebrate and express itself in him in every way that love can.

His new birth from the dead has given us power to become children of God. Through baptism, the 'narrow door to light', we die and are reborn into the freedom of his resurrection, into a life that seeks ever-new ways to express itself in us. We are not locked into either circumstances or our past. The restrictions are not simply removed, but their power to constrain us is broken. We can accept them and live with them for no other reason but love, and they can become for us too the narrow passage to life, because there are many little deaths and rebirths before the final breakthrough.

The Christmas mystery is already the promise of our paschal rebirth in Christ, but the promise is conveyed by the image of childhood. A weary, sophisticated people is recalled to its dignity by the contemplation of a baby. The baby, however, stands for growth. As he himself is committed to the whole project of being fully human and open to God from within manhood, so the promise of new life and rebirth for us is not a permission for childishness or remaining immature. There are paradoxes here. Echoing in our minds is the Lord's warning, 'Unless you change and become like little children, you shall not enter the kingdom of heaven' (cf. Matt. 18.3), yet St Paul rebuked the Corinthians for childishness: 'I could not address you as spiritual men, but as men of the flesh, as babes in Christ. I fed you with milk, not solid food; for you were not ready for it; and even yet you are not ready, for you are still of the flesh' (1 Cor. 3.1–3). Moreover Jesus put very adult challenges to his friends. We are to take up our cross and follow him, to Calvary and to glory; we are to choose, knowing that heaven and hell are in the balance. These are not children's games. The Letter to the Ephesians opens up the perspectives of ultimate Christian maturity, achieved by many together, in organic union with Christ. We are to grow

> until we all attain to the unity of the faith and of the knowledge of the Son of God, to mature manhood, to the measure of the stature of the fulness of Christ; so that we may no longer be children. . . . Rather, speaking the truth in love, we are to grow up in every way into him who is the head, into Christ, from whom the whole body, joined and knit together by every joint with which it is supplied . . . makes bodily growth and upbuilds itself in love.
> (Eph. 4.13-16)

The paradox, like every other paradox in Christian life, comes back to the person of Christ himself. In his childhood there are qualities of sonship which he never lost: trust, openness, simplicity, the need to love and be loved. He never lost them, but he transposed them and lived them anew throughout the experiences of maturity. His openness to and trust in the Father took him through barrier after barrier with the singleminded simplicity of headlong love; his need to express in human relationships the love that longed for people drove him to endless availability, friendship and compassion, and in the end to that sharing of himself which is sacramentally embodied in the Eucharist: the broken bread, the given body, the outpoured life.

Our new birth as sons and daughters of God is a share in Christ's sonship, and we are therefore invited by the Christmas mystery to explore the implications of it as he did. Obedience and simplicity are supposed to be 'natural' to childhood; whether they are or not there is a different obedience and a different simplicity in adult love, the fruit not of natural condition but of deliberate choices made in the power of the Spirit of sonship. In the Spirit we know our Father and cry 'Abba', recognizing the love that unreservedly offers itself and asks to be met by nothing less than unconditional surrender. In prayer we feel the strong central pull which draws every element in our lives into alignment and unity, and so we find a simplicity amid the clutter. We want only one thing, God's will; this is not the same as a child's simplicity but is its adult counterpart, the 'single eye' of the Gospel, the 'purity of heart' of which the ancients spoke, the inner integrity and unity of a person who stands before God in truth and will seek nothing apart from his will. This is not the 'innocence' of childhood, for it is accompanied by a keen sense of sinfulness; but it is part of the way we live out our sonship. We are invited by the gift of Christmas to enter into Jesus's experience of the Father.

This Christmas birth that leads him into it is the echo in time of the Son's eternal birth from the Father, in that Trinity where each is for the others. This means that our exploring of the implications of sonship cannot be only a solitary adventure, however much the occasional patch of solitude in our lives may help us to go deeper in the search. There is often a curve in the human person's growth towards maturity. We begin with the *participation mystique* of womb-life, when the child's being is locked into that of its mother. Birth is a preliminary separation, but the close dependence continues through the early years. Growth towards adulthood usually involves a personal assertion of separateness and independence; then the young man or woman leaves home, sets out on a career, marries, has children, achieves something. There is a strong, fairly confident, self-conscious grown-upness. Yet further growth, deepening and genuine self-discovery will generally lead him or her to a recognition of need, the need for other persons, for some kind of community and exchange. The individuation process documented by C. G. Jung leads a person to live from his or her deep centre, and yet to find there not simply solitude but capacity for communion. It is the same in Christian growth. The life is of its essence an exchange, 'light caught from a leaping flame'. Because it is the life of the Trinity it is giving and receiving, flow and reflow, a dance of love. Maturity is found not in isolation but in willing communion, in the organic fellowship of the Body of Christ.

The sheer physical reality of our new being 'in Christ' is the central conviction of Paul's teaching, so it is not surprising that he resorts to the image of birth. In 1 Corinthians 4.15 he speaks of himself as a father who has begotten his converts in Christ Jesus through the gospel; in Galatians 4.19 he has not only the image of himself as a mother, but what looks like a baffling mixed metaphor: 'My little children, with whom I am again in travail until Christ be formed in you!' Perhaps it is an abrupt switch: Paul has laboriously brought forth his Galatian converts, and now agonizes as he watches the slowness of Christ's full development in them. They now seem to be the pregnant mothers.

However it may be about Paul's metaphors, the idea of God's people as mother of the Messiah, or of messianic salvation, is well rooted in both Old and New Testaments.

The failed childbearing of Isaiah 26.18 has already been mentioned in Chapter 1:

> We were with child, we writhed,
> we have as it were brought forth wind.
> We have wrought no deliverance in the earth.

But in Isaiah 66.7 the situation is different:

> Before she was in labour she gave birth;
> before her pain came upon her she was delivered of a son.

The reference is probably to the new people, not to the person of the Messiah, and the imagery evokes the sudden, unexpected character of the birth; the usual presuppositions are not there. In the Last Supper discourse recorded by John, Jesus alludes to these Isaian passages, speaking of his approaching death and resurrection as a painful birth leading to joy:

> When a woman is in travail she has sorrow, because her hour has come; but when she is delivered of the child, she no longer remembers the anguish, for joy that a child is born into the world. So you have sorrow now, but I will see you again and your hearts will rejoice, and no one will take your joy from you.
> (John 16.21–2)

His passion is the painful bearing of the new world, and his apostles represent the new messianic people which is to bring forth the risen Christ, the 'first-born from the dead'. They are the 'remnant' in which Israel has fulfilled its vocation.

In the Book of Revelation the image returns, more sharply focused; again we meet a representative woman, who is

> clothed with the sun, with the moon under her feet, and on her head a crown of twelve stars; she was with child and she cried out in her pangs of birth, in anguish for delivery . . . . And the dragon stood before the woman who was about to bear a child, that he might devour her child when she brought it forth; she brought forth a male child, one who is

61

> to rule all the nations with a rod of iron, but her child was caught up to God and to his throne, and the woman fled into the wilderness, where she has a place prepared by God, in which to be nourished.
> (Rev. 12.1–6)

This woman seems to be at first Israel, the people of promise giving birth to its Messiah; but then the Church, the new people which is still a pilgrim on earth and a desert-traveller after the 'Child' has been glorified.

It is not necessary to read any direct allusion to Mary into this text of Revelation, but the theology of both John and Luke does suggest a kind of reciprocal inclusion between Mary and the Church. At the beginning of the story of the incarnation the Church is present in Mary, like a seed. Later, Mary is present in the Church. All along she typifies and realizes the Church, and she stands also for the physical, literal, down-to-earth presence of the mystery of Christ in each one of us. The Church must bring forth Christ to the world in every age and culture; the Church must show his face anew to mankind in every incarnation of his presence among men. But the Church is people, and the new birth of Christ to the world will happen only in the measure that we allow him to penetrate our personal lives, take shape in us, 'be formed in us', as Paul exhorted his Galatians. So we are back again to Paul's mixed metaphor, and we cannot get away from it. Our union with Christ is too complete to admit of tidy statement. We can give life to others, give Christ to others, only in so far as by faith and by sharing his paschal death we come to new birth in him.

The word 'new' has tremendous resonances in Christianity. Christ brings us a new covenant, a new birth, a new commandment of love and the new wine of Eucharist; we are formed into one new man in him, we sing the new song of the redeemed, and we await a new Jerusalem, a new heaven and a new earth.[15] This renewal is wholly God's work, but it is not carried through without our consent. It takes courage and humility to let go of the old and allow yourself to be created anew. There are hints of this in various prayers of the

Roman liturgy that ask God to rid us of 'the contagion of the old thing'[16] or, even more graphically, 'any sneaking return of our old nature'.[17] We ask to be hollowed out, emptied out, to have 'space in us for holy newness' (*capaces sanctae novitatis*); it echoes the old idea of the mystics, that the human person becomes *capax Dei* by grace, able to receive the self-giving God. A classic prayer of Christmas time asks:

> Almighty God, we beg you to grant that we who are held fast in ancient servitude under the yoke of sin may be set free by your only Son's new birth in the flesh.

The real 'new thing' is Easter, but inevitably the Easter notes keep breaking in at Christmas. A traditional response at Christmas Matins sums it up: 'Today the dawn of a new redemption has broken upon us, a restoration ordained from of old, a joy that will have no end.'

In the child who is one with God and yet one with us there is two-way communication. The Greek Fathers liked to say that God became man to make men gods, and this idea is echoed in a liturgical prayer attributed to St Leo:

> O God you created man most wonderfully but still more wonderfully have renewed him; grant that we may become sharers in his divine nature, who has deigned to share our humanity.

It is an exchange, a bargain almost, as the liturgy for New Year's Day sings: 'O marvellous exchange! Man's Creator has taken manhood from a virgin, and endowed us with his godhead!'

There is a springlike quality about Christmas, and even about its starlit preparation in Advent, for all the wintry atmosphere which gives it character. It is not like the spring of Lent and Easter, for the mood is different, but it is real. On the day when the Gospel of Mary's Visitation to Elizabeth is read, the Old Testament reading which precedes it catches the springlike mood; yet this is the 21 December, the winter solstice! The contrast is perfect:

> I hear my Beloved.
> See how he comes

> leaping upon the mountains,
> bounding over the hills.
> My Beloved is like a gazelle,
> like a young stag.
> See where he stands
> behind our wall.
> He looks in at the window,
> he peers through the lattice.
> My Beloved lifts up his voice,
> he says to me,
> 'Come then, my love,
> my lovely one, come.
> For see, winter is past,
> the rains are over and gone.
> The flowers appear on the earth.
> The season of glad songs has come,
> the cooing of the turtledove is heard
> in our land.
> The fig tree is forming its first figs
> and the blossoming vines give out their fragrance.
> Come then, my love,
> my lovely one, come.'
> (Song of Sol. 2.8-13, JB)

He is humankind's Lover, the Beyond who stands behind the barrier, asking for love. From the incarnation the Lover is in the world, and the process of its transformation has begun. Christmas is a promise, spring a sign of it, Easter its triumph in Christ's humanity. The process continues as human beings consent to die and to be new-born in him; it spreads from spirit to matter and ultimately to that transformation of all matter for which the cosmos groans in travail, awaiting the last breakthrough, when 'the creation itself will be set free from its bondage to decay and obtain the glorious liberty of the children of God' (Rom. 8.21). That will be the work of another and final 'coming of the Lord', but the comings we know already point to it.

5   Listening to the Word

If the lost word is lost, if the spent word is spent
If the unheard, unspoken
Word is unspoken, unheard;
Still is the unspoken word, the Word unheard,
The Word without a word, the Word within
The world and for the world;
And the light shone in darkness and
Against the Word the unstilled world still whirled
About the centre of the silent Word.

     O my people, what have I done unto thee.

Where shall the word be found, where will the word
Resound? Not here, there is not enough silence
Not on the sea or on the islands, not
On the mainland, in the desert or on the rain land,
For those who walk in darkness
Both in the day time and in the night time
The right time and the right place are not here
No place of grace for those who avoid the face
No time to rejoice for those who walk among noise and deny the
    voice.[1]

Personal communication, the kind of speaking by which someone reveals and commits himself, requires a listener. It does not work as a simple monologue. Anyone who has tried to continue a phone conversation after the other person has hung up, or to go on writing letters to someone who never replies, or to talk in a truly human way to someone who has closed his mind and is stone-walling, is aware of this simple fact. Genuinely personal speech is not possible unless both parties involved are in some degree committing themselves. We cannot really speak unless there is receptivity and response; even God cannot. Nor can we really listen to another person without openness, acceptance, humility and something akin to love. Silence can be very different according to our attitude; it can convey disapproval, snubbing the speaker as effectively as a sharp word, or it can be healing and creative, giving the other confidence that he or she is understood. Together, only together, we can rise to truth, vision and communion.

All the beauty and riches that open to us through communication with other persons are possible because God has made us in his image. The Greeks defined man as 'a living thing that speaks'. We speak through verbal exchange, through body-language of manifold variety, through literature, art and music, through silent presence to one another, and through living truthfully in the fellowship of love that binds us together in a common humanity and a common destiny. This destiny is fellowship with the God who is communion, and with one another in him.

Our God is a God who gives himself; that is his glory. From all eternity he dwells in unapproachable light, yet he comes to find us, to call us and offer his friendship, and to ask for ours. His trinitarian glory is self-giving love, and it overflows, as is the way with love; so he is glorified not by remaining inaccessible but by self-communication. This is what Revelation is: God speaking, not to present us with a list of truths we must believe or rules we must obey, but to utter *himself*.

He formed Israel, the People of the Word. Partially, fitfully they listened, but often they were deaf and didn't want to know. God's word of self-giving love was not truly heard until it was received in the human mind of Jesus Christ. Jesus is the first listener. The word is heard elsewhere – in the Church and in our own hearts – only because it is first heard there. God gives himself, makes himself known as the one who wants to be known, not in some external way only but in the deepest, most personal, most human centre of our race, in the mind and heart of Jesus Christ. Self-giving. self-revealing God meets self-giving, responding, participating, receptive man. God's desire to love and give himself to mankind was consummated there, because Jesus let it happen. This is revelatory communion.

Jesus's mind was human. He is one with us not only in bodily nature but precisely where we are most human, in our minds. 'What Christ did not assume has not been healed', the Fathers used to say, certain that everything human in us has become his. The 'human nature' of the Word made flesh is a free, active, spiritual being who can stand before God in genuinely responsive attitudes of prayer, obedience and love, supremely personal in *our* sense.[2] Jesus can listen to God, as a man listens.

Part of being human as we understand it is that man is not a static, complete reality but dynamic and emergent. He is someone who breaks into the world, chooses, decides, takes responsibility for his decisions, discovers himself and becomes himself through encounter with others and through living experience. I am most truly described in terms of what I am capable of becoming. I am growing; I am half-baked. Existentialist philosophers have helped us to think in this way, but the biblical writers thought similarly. Only in the perspective of the Last Things can someone or something be truly known. In this too Jesus is with us, inside our most human experience. He had to grow and discover; he had to 'learn obedience through the things he suffered' (cf. Heb. 5.8). And yet he is God.

We are never going to understand this mystery, in the sense of dominating it and exhausting its content, because a mystery in the theological sense is not a puzzle or problem to be solved; it is a communication of God's reality to be lived with and adored. But this does not dispense us from using our intelligence as far as it will take us, and the best model we have in the present instance is our experience of the Creator–creature relationship at its highest: the relationship between God and a free, spiritual being in grace. Only God can constitute something in being which is really distinct from himself, autonomous and free, yet increases in freedom and responsibility in direct ratio to its nearness to God and dependence on him. Our experience of 'creating' is not like this; either the product is under our control but not free, or it is free (like a child) but escapes our control. The Jewish and Christian understanding of God as Creator is something other.The freedom of the creature is not destroyed or absorbed by being handed over to God; on the contrary, because I am a created person I become more personal, more free, more myself and more real in proportion to my closeness to God. This experience is for us fragmentary, and covers only the best areas in our lives. For Jesus it is total. Godhead did not swamp or cramp that most marvellous part of creation, his human mind.

To make this comparison between Jesus and ourselves is not to deny the uniqueness of the incarnation, or to make the difference between Christ's relationship to God and ours merely one of degree. That Christ is unique mystery does not mean that he is unrelated to everything else in creation; he is the supreme self-giving towards which God's creative, saving plans were directed from the beginning. His incarnation is not a correction or an afterthought in a world already complete. He is the first-born of all creation.

Jesus's mind, then, was human, and he needed to grow humanly in understanding, in maturity and wisdom, as we do, and especially in the greatest and deepest things of his life. This means that he had to grow above all in discovering the Father as his Father, as the one who loved him. Traditional theology holds that Jesus knew from the first that he was Son of God; there are good reasons for thinking that he must have known. But we can 'know' things at different levels, and some of the deepest and most important things we know are not immediately available at the level of everyday words and concepts. If you ask a newly married woman how she knows that her husband loves her she may wax incoherent, but not because she does not know it. If you ask one of God's lovers how he knows that God loves him you are unlikely to get a logically satisfying reply. It takes you all your life to discover the meaning of the simple statement 'God loves *you*', yet you may have known it for as long as you can remember. This gives us some light on Jesus. He knew he was Son, but this cannot have been like registering a simple fact. A person knows himself in a way quite different from the way he knows other persons and things; he implicitly knows and affirms himself in the knowing of anything else. Jesus cannot have come to know God, in the sense of knowing himself as Son and the Father as his Father, simply by acquiring knowledge from outside; it was far more immediate and intuitive than that. All the same, he did need time and experience of external things in order to get to grips with what he knew, to translate his intuitive knowledge into something his mind could grasp. He had to wrestle with the mystery of himself and his sonship. He needed time to come to terms with the mysterious love that was calling to him, claiming him, addressing him through every experience and at every turn in the road. He needed to listen and listen and listen to the Father's word of love to him, 'You are my Son, my beloved'. Since being human was for him, as for us, an emerging, unfolding reality, he cannot have heard that word as a single, once-for-all event. He had to hear it with the mind of a small child,[3] then a young boy, then a man; and he had to respond from where he was. He had to grow into, live his way into, what it meant to be the Son, what it meant that the Father loved him like that. He is the Father's Word made man, but as man he had to listen to that Word.

It was a process of discovery. In our lives experience, especially experience of human relationships, interacts with prayer, and as this happens a person comes to understand and accept himself. This must have been true for Jesus as well; relationships and prayer were important ways in which he heard the Father's word to him. His relationship with his mother must have been one of the greatest joys of his life, a steady strength and a growing, maturing reality between them, as each of them searched for the way forward. We tend to think less of his relationship to Joseph, but apart from giving the special protection to mother and child which they needed in the early years, Joseph had an essential role in providing for Jesus the male relationship he needed, to teach him how to be a man and to be for him a special sacrament of his Father's love. In adult life it was the same; Jesus needed friendship and understanding. He needed friends not only as an emotional support and a group of allies in his work, but as part of his own search. When he was struggling to understand he needed people to talk to, other minds to respond and react to his, friends with whom he could share his vision.

All this must have continually interacted with his prayer, because prayer is always wedded to experience. He needed to pray; the need was sometimes more imperative than the need to sleep. We know that the word 'Abba' came readily, because it was remembered by the Church when it no longer spoke Aramaic, but there must also have been a need simply to expose himself wordlessly to the Father, to be silent, to let the reality of the relationship take over and claim him. This is where, above all, there took place that communion between God and humankind which we call Revelation. When Jesus prayed, God's desire to give himself in love was consummated. Within our race there was perfect receptivity. God could give himself to man, because Jesus was willing; the word was spoken and listened to. The Word made flesh was listening to the Word, and listening as one of us. This is revelatory communion, and it takes place still in the glorified mind of Jesus.

As he grew throughout his life his prayer grew with him, interacting all the time with his human discovery of life, persons, joy and suffering, and confronting him in his maturing love and understanding with the Father's love and his own reality as Son. All along he had to work it out in human terms; 'Son though he was, he learned obedience through the things he suffered'.

There were key moments, the leap of understanding, the sudden insight, the coming together of previously unrelated pieces of knowledge. The human mind works that way: a text you have heard or read hundreds of times hits you one day with a new meaning; or someone speaks to you and lights up far more than is evident from the words, because they formulate what was vaguely there in your mind without your realizing it. It seems that Jesus's baptism was one of these moments of breakthrough; he heard the Father speak his love that day. 'You are my Son, my

Beloved, my Servant': he knew it already, but now he knew it in a different way.[4]

Perhaps it is significant that the Synoptics follow this story immediately with that of Jesus's long fast in the desert and his temptations. He was the new Israel, certainly, God's Israel, recapitulating his people's experience with the Lord of the wilderness; but he was not play-acting. Events of 'theological significance' in Jesus's life always emerged from a real human situation demanding imaginative human response. At that moment, after the messianic experience of his baptism, he absolutely needed to be alone with the Father; he needed that unshielded exposure to God in the desert. The desert is the place where God's word is listened to by those freed from irrelevancies. Like his forbears, he also experienced there a confrontation with evil. 'If you are the Son of God. . .'; this is the refrain of the temptations. *If* you are. . . . Perhaps the reality of his experience is being called in question. Was that intuition of love real? Can you really trust it? Sensible people don't take risks like that; better to make sure of success, secure yourself, insure yourself against loss. . . . We know what this means; anyone who prays knows it well. Jesus refused the suggestions, replied with the scriptural word of God,[5] and chose to commit himself to the reality of the word of love he had heard. He staked his all on the Father's faithfulness, and this is not once only but repeatedly. The story of the temptations is a synthesis of many an occasion when he chose to obey his Father, chose to seek the meaning of his life in the Father's love.

Still in the months that followed there was ignorance and risk, and the continual search for meaning. He had to listen in prayer and sensitize himself, walk in what light he had, try out something and fail, let go of his own plans in order to be available for the Father's, transcend his own limitations and step out in courageous unknowing because the Father said 'Come'. There is an image of this in the Gospels when Peter steps out of the comparative security of the boat, not yet knowing that the water will hold him up, simply because Jesus says 'Come'. Jesus himself had to step out many times from what was familiar and controllable, because the Father was saying 'Come'. He practised a great deal for the final leap: 'Father, into your hands I commit my spirit.' Each time he was choosing to let the Father's love be his whole meaning, and each time there was a little death as he let go of the earlier pattern and was reborn to something new.

The miracles could have been such leaps. Confronted with people suffering through sickness, hunger, grief or bereavement, Jesus was moved with all the compassion natural to a mature and highly passionate human being. But the extremity of the situation proclaimed man's need for God. It was an open, crying wound calling for the salvation which will ultimately transfigure not only our spirits but also our bodies and the cosmos, and so it challenged Jesus to be, intensely, what he was: a man identified with the human lot and yet wholly open to God within it. It challenged him in all the depth and breadth of his humanity to be the Son, consciously, willingly, with all the force of his love, with all that being Son meant of demand and gift. He surrendered to the Father's love and it went through him as compassionate, healing power. God and man danced together as their loves met. When other persons were involved, Jesus took advantage of their vulnerability at those moments, inviting them to step with him into the same trust-relationship with the Father: the blind, the lepers, the sinful, the apostles who were told to distribute the loaves without being able to see before beginning that the handful was going to stretch. They, and we, are invited by Jesus to share his experience of being Son, to entrust ourselves with him into the Father's hands, to break through a barrier to the Lover who stands beyond it. When people do so, the reality of the Kingdom is there, fleetingly and by anticipation. We cannot yet habitually live in that Kingdom, but its signs escape the boundaries of time and show through in a world still in servitude to evil. So when John the Baptist sent his disciples to Jesus, asking, 'Are you he who is to come, or have we still to look for someone else?', Jesus pointed to these distant early-warning signals of the inbreaking Kingdom: 'Go and tell John what you hear and see: the blind receive their sight and the lame walk, lepers are cleansed and the deaf hear, and the dead are raised up, and the poor have the good news preached to them' (Matt. 11.4-5).

His response to his vocation was a continual choosing anew, as ours is, in deeper understanding and maturing freedom. He had to let go of his chances of success, because the Father said, 'Not that way', and he responded, 'Father, into your hands. . . .' What he was being asked, what the word to which he listened was telling him, was to let the Father's love be the entire, all-sufficient meaning of his life. As he steadily committed himself and worked out the human consequences of being Son, the Father's word of love became increasingly mysterious.

> The road,
> You shall follow it.
>
> The fun,
> You shall forget it.
>
> The cup,
> You shall empty it.
>
> The pain,
> You shall conceal it.
>
> The truth,
> You shall be told it.
>
> The end,
> You shall endure it.[6]

In the end the word to which he was listening had to be for him the word of the cross. Externally it had to be, because his message and claims were seen to be an absolute challenge to a religious establishment which, unless it were prepared to accept the unique authority of Jesus and take the consequences for its own privileged status, was bound to react by putting him out of the way as an imposter and a threat. Internally too there was something necessary about his death, something he had to consummate as man that required his act of dying. In Gethsemane he was faced with the ultimate choice. He was asked to let go of everything, every other source of meaning, his work and success, his future, his life itself. He faced the total collapse of all he had lived for and tried to do. The cross was the destruction of all meaning; there was nothing left now except the Father's mysterious word, the baffling love that beckoned that way. He said 'Yes' once more, and worked it out through the passion. His self-commitment into the Father's hands entailed, with terrible irony, self-commitment into the hands of men.

On the cross his sonship was made humanly perfect. He stayed open to those he claimed as brothers, even in their capacity of torturers: 'Father, forgive them. . . .' (Luke 23.34). In agony and darkness he expressed his final self-surrender to his Father: 'Father, into your hands I commit my spirit.' The work of translating the reality of divine sonship into human terms was consummated. Hidden by the pain, desolation and degradation, his obedient dying was a Godlike act. Self-giving, self-emptying love, an ecstasy of unreserved giving in joy, is characteristic of trinitarian relationships. It is the glory of God to give, holding nothing back. In his dying Jesus expressed this relationship in ultimate human maturity; as Son made man he was finally open and responsive to the Father's word, 'You are my Son'.

The resurrection is the other face of this obedient surrender. It is not simply the reversal of what went before, though in certain respects it is that; it is the full revelation of what went before, the open manifestation of the glory of the love between Father and Son. The resurrection is the Father's acceptance of the Son's gift, and the penetration by the Spirit of their mutual love into every fibre of Jesus's body and mind, into every dimension of the manhood which had become the means of expressing love. We think more readily of his risen body, but his mind is glorified too. He has heard the Father's word with his whole being. Son though he was all along, he learned obedience and grew to perfect, achieved freedom by the things he suffered. He is Son now to the utmost depths of his human psyche:

What God promised to the fathers, this he has fulfilled. . .
by raising Jesus; as also it is written in the second psalm,
> 'Thou art my Son,
> today I have begotten thee'.

(Acts 13.32-3)

No last barrier of mortality remained between his glorified mind and the word of God. At last he became the place of revelatory communion in its fullness. For all eternity, and therefore *now*, God's revelation is received perfectly in the human mind of Jesus. He is listening now. He is now and for ever the complete openness of our finite being towards God, the Creator–creature relationship at its most real. The Lover is with the Beloved and all barriers down.

Yet glorified as he is, Jesus is still with us on our pilgrimage, and wants to share his Easter understanding with the Church as he travels with us down the long road of history. He wants to lead us into his own experience of the Father, into that 'knowing' between Father and Son which needed Easter to make it perfect in Christ's manhood. The story in Luke 24 of the disciples going to Emmaus is a work of genius. The two travellers are not just two people who happened to be there that night; they are the Church, they are you and I, because this is Luke's inspired picture of how things are in the Easter Church, the Church of Word and Sacrament: the long journey, the distress and bewilderment, the knowing yet not knowing, the patient tenderness of Christ as he tries to open their minds to understand the Scriptures, their burning hearts, their eventual recognition that they have indeed known the Lord in the breaking of the bread of the Word and the bread of Eucharist. The word is not always clarifying; it is mysterious, because it is the presence and self-communication of God. It is not always informative; it is performative, creative: changing and converting and renewing us. And there is something about the journey, the long experience of the road, that makes us able to hear it.

'We had hoped,' say the travellers to the Lord. 'We had hoped that things would go like this. . . .' We had our plans, but now. . . . Easter is utterly disconcerting, because it is the power and mystery of God taking hold of our frail mortality, our limited hopes. 'Don't you see,' their unrecognized fellow-pilgrim asks them. Don't you see that it had to be like that? Was it not written? Isn't it what all the Scriptures are about, from end to end? Don't you understand that the Christ had to suffer and so enter into his glory? Don't you understand that it can't be otherwise for you? You have to jettison your small plans, because the Father's plans for you are unthinkably greater and more wonderful. You have to leap into his hands, say an unconditional 'Yes' and be born anew. His love exceeds all that you deserve or even desire.

This word to which we listen in the Easter Christ, and with him, is not a word coming from outside ourselves, an alien thing. It is spoken in the centre of our being, because of the gift of the Spirit to us from the Easter Christ. The Spirit opens our hearts from within to receive the word, shapes our minds to the mind of Christ, drags us away from what is merely our own, unselfs us, makes us love the Father's will, and so is at the heart of both our listening and our prayer. All our listening is done in the Easter Christ, through the gift of the Spirit who makes us listeners, because sons.

We have to wait in obedience, listening with an obedient heart to the Father's word, because only the obedient heart can truly listen. If we have reservations, areas in our lives into which we are unwilling to admit God, we shall not be able to hear. The root of our prayer and of our whole life with God is an unconditional 'Yes' that does not necessarily understand all the time what is going on, but is still given. We have to be prepared to trust him and obey, unconditionally and all the time, in every area of our lives, in small things as well as great. This is the condition for contemplative prayer. Obedience, love and prayer almost coincide; at any rate they are inseparable.

This means that we have to be non-selective about where we hear the word of God. The word not only heals and comforts; it also judges and convicts, rebukes and shames us, and there are some places and occasions where we would rather not hear it. But if we try to be selective we immediately fall away from obedience and purity of heart, and that means creeping deafness. If you keep on listening to God's word of love in your life, listening in purity of heart and obedience, you find that you come to hear it everywhere, often through very unexpected channels. Are you prepared, for instance, to hear it in disappointment, humiliation, failure and frustration? Or in the daily realities of living with other people?

We listen in our own hearts, individually, in prayer and experience. We listen also as a people, gathered together by the Spirit. There are three special 'places' for listening which in some way give the key to all the rest: the word comes to us through Scripture, through people and the human condition, and in personal prayer.

The Bible was born of the Spirit's action passing through the shared faith of a community, God's people. The whole life of this people was a word of God. The word was heard, experienced as dynamic action, suffered, rejoiced in, prayed over, mulled over and passed on; it was a river of life. There was a deposit from the river: here and there a prophet or a sage or a scribe was raised up who embodied his people's faith in a special way, who listened to God within the heart of that people and articulated the experience in words which could be repeated and written.[7] It was the same with the birth of the New Testament from the life and faith of the first Christian generations, except that the time-span was shorter and the Word was now a man whom they had seen with their eyes and touched with their hands.

When we read in faith those articulated words, born from experience of God amid a praying, believing community, we read or listen to them as members of a praying, believing community, even if we are physically alone. We are the holy assembly gathered by the same Spirit who spoke through the prophets; the Word is alive and powerful for us as for them, and we travel by it to an experience of God. The experience is both individual and communal, necessarily both. Your personal listening in your prayer and your life deepens and fertilizes the listening that is done by the Body, but the faith of that Body supports and illumines and enriches your own. The scriptural word finds its proper intelligibility in a community of faith.

The shared listening of a community of faith is an educative factor of immense significance, particularly when its members are gathered for prayer. Reverence, humility and a sense of God's holiness can be communicated to us by the very bearing of those who read or listen to the word of God with us. The gospel is mediated to us as they read it: the Good News comes to me through the mind and voice of the one who proclaims it, and that means through the prayer and experience and understanding and grace of the one who proclaims it. I need other people to proclaim the Good News to me by the way they pray and read and live. There is a communication of faith as we listen together to God; we are aware of the call to pray more deeply, and we feel the contemplative pull.

Between the simplest believer and the highest mystic the same communion in faith holds. The great Christian mystics are not some in-group with access to special mysteries; they are baptized men and women who have fed on the same vital word, and allowed the Easter Christ to take them the whole way. The communication of faith is not only horizontal, between contemporaries; it spans generations. The minds and lives of Christians all down the ages, the minds of the saints and mystics and of the humble, heroic, unknown believers of every age and place, have been formed and fertilized by the same seed of the word.

As you listen, you recognize your own story. You listen from the inside; you have the key. It is no alien story of long ago in which we might take a polite but detached interest; rather, as Nathan said to David, 'Thou art the man!' (cf. 2 Sam. 12.1-15). Your own personal life with God, the touches of his love in your experience, the chaos of your prayer or your work, your need of his mercy and consciousness of his grace – all this is genuinely, objectively, a stage in the salvation history to which you are listening. Not only are you part of it as a late-comer in the drama; you also recognize the signs you know, the experiences you share, as they occur in the earlier stages. You are aware of call and response in your own story, of sin and repentance, the summons to conversion and discipleship, the promise and the ever-present hope. The story to which you listen in Scripture and your own life as you live it are *mutually* illuminating: you can hear the word in Scripture because you know the hidden word in your life, but it is the scriptural word which is a lamp for your steps and a light for your path as you go back again to the task of living. This is no make-believe. 'Today, if you hear his voice, harden not your hearts.'[8]

I need people to be word-bearers, prophets, to me. Even Jesus did. The friends who tried to understand, the crowds who pressed on him and drained him, were part of his Father's word to him, and it took all his love and generosity to stay open to that word. His vocation as universal Saviour and first-born of many brethren implied a relationship of personal availability and openness to every human being, but this relationship cannot have been a ready-made role which he simply had to assume. He had to live his way into it humanly, just as he had to live his way into being the Father's Son in human terms. He had to work for it, as we do, because human maturity in any sense other than the physical does have to be worked for. Nevertheless it was not all heroic giving, all one-way. Nobody can be as humanly open and generous in self-giving as Jesus was without receiving a great deal himself. He needed people in order to learn, humanly, how to love. He needed their need, and he needed their response as he tried to understand. 'Who do men say that I am? And who do *you* say that I am?' (cf. Mark 8.27,29). That dialogue is another instance of a theologically significant event which must, all the same, have had thoroughly credible, human psychological roots. In people's response to him he discovered himself and learned to know the Father. In speaking to them, speaking the very word he had received from the Father, he heard that word more truly himself.

Within the give and take of life together we too hear the Father's word, because Jesus has so thoroughly committed himself to being present within it. At the last supper his love drove him to wash the disciples' feet, in the guise of a slave. Peter protested at the unseemliness, but Jesus warned him, 'If I do not wash you, you have no part in me' (John 13.8). He went on, 'If I then, your Lord and Teacher, have washed your feet, you also ought to wash one another's feet' (John 13.14). His action was a symbolic expression of the humble, serviceable love which he bore them, which God bears us, which we have to bear one another. It is the condition of 'having part with' him. In bearing the weaknesses of others and being ourselves borne with, in compassion and humble, serviceable love, in forgiving and being forgiven, in sharing life and thought and joy and work, in the whole business of living together we share his Easter life, we know his presence and we hear the Lord's word. The human condition is itself a privileged place for listening.

The listening which can go on all day amid a variety of occupations is concentrated when we give up time to be alone with God in prayer. Prayer is an exposure to the reality of God. For those who pray regularly the time may come fairly soon when particular thoughts or words no longer seem to help. Prayer seems to have gone dead. The relationship is moving into a new phase, and you have to learn to change gear. At other times you may be able to find as much inspiration as ever in the Scriptures, in thinking about God and in the experiences that generally mediate his word to you, but when you try any of this in the time of prayer, you have the impression that this and real prayer are mutually exclusive. To be spending the time on that is somehow to dodge the issue. This can be a distressing and disconcerting experience, but it may be another 'creative disintegration' and the way through to contemplative prayer.

Provided that you are refusing God nothing, you can probably trust the inclination to let it ride a bit. Wait in silence, attentiveness, stillness, just aware of God in some dim way and of your need of him, but without particular efforts to formulate ideas or words, except perhaps just to bring yourself gently back when you stray. It is baffling and disconcerting, but in some way all-important to you to stay there like that in darkness and quiet.

You are exposed in your truth to the God who made you – who is making you now – and, amazingly, he accepts you and loves you as you are. You are truly poor, you have no merits to list, no progress, no achievements; yet you are unconditionally loved. You are secure; you cannot fall any further, because you are at rock-bottom already. You have no meaning in any achievement, role or status of your own: your whole meaning is in your Father's love for you.

This is real inner poverty, the daily need to be converted and begin again; but it is also real security, the security in love we need if we are to be open to change, free enough in heart to let go of anything, anything at all, when the Spirit calls us on. The Spirit who makes us cry 'Abba' is not a child's comforter. He brings us to the brink of the abyss of love where we are asked, Do you *dare* to have nothing but the Father's love? This is what sonship is about, the sonship which is a sharing in Christ's Easter experience. You are being invited to be unshielded against the Father's love. You are not to have any insurance policy against the living God. And we are 'sore adread, lest having him we must have nought beside'.[9]

You are moving from the state of knowing about God to knowing God, from the state where you could have fairly clear ideas and feel you were in control of them, where the word was something your mind could objectify and grasp, to the state where you are simply exposed to God, directly in contact with him through faith and hope and love. It is very uncomfortable, and you gasp for air. His word is not clarifying but utterly mysterious. Yet it is love. You have to abide in quiet, doing your best to stay in that love, whether he leaves you in empty dullness, or a prey to distractions, or enfolds you with some sense of his presence and reality. Just stay there, steadfastly trusting, refusing to clutch at anything less. There is real unknowing: you honestly do not know whether you are on the map or not, whether this business you call your prayer is genuine or not. Often it seems to have been a non-event. Guarantees of that kind – the certainty that you are praying or have prayed – are part of what you have given up. You can only go on trusting him.

You want to surrender unconditionally to his love, yet you feel that you never quite pull it off. Or you seem to, and then fall away again from the reality which is what you most deeply want. At death you will make the surrender unconditionally and unambiguously. Through all the weakness you will say, 'Father, into your hands I commit my spirit'. Your assimilation to the Easter Christ will be complete, and death will be the best part of living, the thing for which you have been practising.

To listen inwardly to the word of love in this direct, personal, unshielded way requires silence of heart. We have to do all we can to achieve this, to take sensible, practical measures like the choice of a suitable time and place, and perhaps some kind of preparation before prayer to quieten our minds, if that is feasible. Then within prayer we may find it helpful to quieten our imagination and active thinking by using some short word repeatedly, perhaps the name 'Jesus', or any other word like 'God' or 'love'; *The Cloud of Unknowing* is very good on this, as on everything else connected with contemplative prayer, and says it ought to be a one-syllabled word! When distractions do come we should not worry, but just ignore them as far as possible; *The Cloud* again says that you should 'look over their shoulders' at that which is beyond them, God, or, if all else fails, 'yield yourself to God in the hands of your enemies' like one defeated in battle but handed over to *him*.[10] Many of these distractions are only superficial wandering of the imagination, which does not touch the deep, steady set of the will towards God. In ordinary human encounters you can continue to attend to someone you love, with whom you are conversing, even though at a superficial level you are also aware of a clock ticking, or the traffic outside in the street, or the dog jumping around.

The deepest, most real inner silence before God is not mere vacuity, not a simple absence of distractions, but something far more positive. God did not make us to be mental vacuums, he made us volatile and suggestible and he evidently likes us so. There is a deeper silence which accepts it all: accepts yourself, your make-up, your whole being from his hands as a gift of love. It is an acquiescence in his creative word, 'Let there be you' – you as you are. So you stand before him in the truth of your being, poor and weak but lovable and loved, and your silence before him is the stilling of passion, the stilling of self-will, rebellion, resentment and anxiety. Your inner life is still before him like the sea before Christ when he stood up in the boat and said, 'Peace, be still!' (Mark 4.39). It recognized its Lord and there was a great calm. So it is with us. He is Lord of the turmoil, and it is calmed into one single, simple consent to his love.

'The word is very near to you, it is in your mouth and in your heart.'[11] Nearer even than that, because you yourself are his creative word of love. You know him and can listen to him because you are his image, his ikon, because he has mirrored himself in your being and his creative word is even now bringing out that likeness, and giving you to yourself. Your obedient listening to his word is at its most fundamental in this humble, loving acceptance of *yourself* as his word.

The word within you is your own centre, your deepest reality and your freedom. It is God's utterance of your new name, the name that reveals to you your destiny and meaning and all that you can become, as Jesus spoke Mary Magdalene's name to her in the garden. There is a growing sense of identification between ourselves and this word, and in this we are sharing, in our fumbling way, in the experience of Jesus. He is the Word, yet as man he had to listen, and still does listen, to the Word that he is. His listening was made perfect in his Easter reality where obedience meant only union, freedom and joy. This is what the gift of the Spirit is, this consciousness of identification with the Word within; this is sonship, and we cannot but cry 'Abba!' Like Jesus, you have to listen and listen. It will take you all your life to hear the Father's word of love for you; indeed, it will take you all your eternity.

6 First-born of all Creation

O Wisdom,
Word of the Most High,
you reach from world's end to world's end.
Strong and gracious is your ordering of all things;
Come,
and teach us to walk the way of discernment.[1]

So vivid and powerful was the experience of the Word among the chosen people, and so unmistakable the Lord's presence in his Word, that some Old Testament texts represented the Word as a personal agent of God, a messenger sent to carry out his will. Two of these passages have been quoted already:

> As the rain and the snow come down from heaven,
> and return not thither but water the earth,
> making it bring forth and sprout,
> giving seed to the sower and bread to the eater,
> so shall my word be that goes forth from my mouth;
> it shall not return to me empty,
> but it shall accomplish that which I purpose,
> and prosper in the thing for which I sent it.
> (Isa. 55.10–11)

And, after a time of great cold,

> He sends forth his word and it melts them:
> at the breath of his mouth the waters flow.
> (Ps. 147.18, Grail)

Occasionally the Word is seen as a healing agent: when Israelites were ill,

> they cried to the Lord in their need
> and he rescued them in their distress.

He sent forth his word to heal them
and saved their life from the grave.
(Ps. 107 (106).19–20, Grail)

A book which emerged among the Hellenized Jews of the
Diaspora, the Wisdom of Solomon, gave the Word a sterner
aspect; it or he was sent to execute God's judgement upon
Egypt at the time of the exodus:

When peaceful silence lay over all,
and night had run the half of her swift course,
down from the heavens, from the royal throne, leapt your
    all-powerful Word;
into the heart of a doomed land the stern warrior leapt.
Carrying your unambiguous command like a sharp sword,
he stood, and filled the universe with death;
he touched the sky, yet trod the earth.[2]

These vivid personifications of the Word of Yahweh are
paralleled by two other figures, his Wisdom and his Spirit. In
various poetic texts of the Old Testament both of these are
also represented as divine envoys. Only when polytheistic
temptations had become a thing of the past could this kind of
personification be safely allowed, but after the exile it was
used with great effect.

Wisdom and the Word are closely associated, for Wisdom
was 'uttered by the mouth of the Most High' (Sir. 24.3). The
themes of Word and Wisdom were part of developing
revelation in later Israel, and they profoundly influenced the
New Testament's presentation of Christ. Wisdom, like the
Word, is therefore a theme in the Church's Advent, and
reaches a climax on 17 December in the famous antiphon *O
Sapientia*, quoted at the head of this chapter. Yahweh's Spirit,
or Wind, or Breath (the same word is used for all three in
Hebrew) was also personified in a few texts, and here again
there is a close connection with the Word. Breath and Word
are parallel powers in the text from Psalm 147 just quoted,
and another psalmist, pondering God's creative wisdom,
draws the same parallel:

> By his word the heavens were made,
> by the breath of his mouth all the stars.
> (Ps. 33 (32).6, Grail)

In all these personifications, whether of Word or Wisdom or Spirit, the thought of creation is seldom far away.

The backdrop to creation, both the old creation and the new, is chaos. The first chapter of Genesis evokes the dark chaos before God's creative word was spoken, 'Let there be light'. Chaos is formless, ugly, sterile, wet and empty. There is nothing, no opening towards life or being is found within it. But God's Wind, or God's Breath, or God's Spirit moves over the dark chaotic waters, and God's Word is uttered to draw into being that which was not. Then comes the poem, a rhythmic account of seven days. The first three are devoted to separation and distinction: light from darkness, upper waters from lower, sea from land. The next three are for furnishing and equipping the empty regions: plants spring up in their beauty and fertility, the day is given its 'great lamp' and the night its 'lesser lamp' and stars, the seas teem, the birds soar and the earth becomes a paradise of animals. At last comes man, God's darling, the man in whose face God can see his own image, the man who can respond to God and be his friend, the man who can be a little providence, a co-creator. On the seventh day God pauses to enjoy it and delight in it all.

The psalmists delighted in it too:

> How great is your name, O Lord our God,
> through all the earth! . . .
> When I see the heavens, the work of your hands,
> the moon and the stars which you arranged,
> what is man that you should keep him in mind,
> mortal man that you care for him?
> Yet you have made him little less than a god;
> with glory and honour you crowned him,
> gave him power over the works of your hand,
> put all things under his feet. . . .
> (Ps. 8.2, 4–7, Grail)

The waters stood higher than the mountains.
At your threat they took to flight;
at the voice of your thunder they fled.
They rose over the mountains and flowed down
to the place which you had appointed.
You set limits they might not pass
lest they return to cover the earth.
You make springs gush forth in the valleys:
they flow in between the hills.
They give drink to all the beasts of the field;
the wild-asses quench their thirst.
On their banks dwell the birds of heaven;
from the branches they sing their song. . . .
How many are your works, O Lord!
In wisdom you have made them all.
The earth is full of your riches.
(Ps. 104 (103).6–12, 24, Grail)

The account in Genesis, which inspired both these psalms, is not a scientific description but an imaginative statement of firm faith. It is concerned not with the 'how' of the creative process but with who, what and why. Greater knowledge of the time needed for the evolution of living creatures, and awareness of the amazing complexity of the symphony that is life, can only increase our wonder; we should be marvelling even more than the psalmists. The unimaginably long climb, first towards life, then towards intelligence, gives us better reason even than they had to pray,

O Lord, you have been our refuge
from one generation to the next.
Before the mountains were born
or the earth or the world brought forth,
you are God, without beginning or end.
(Ps. 90 (89).1–2, Grail)

Or again,

It was you who created my being,
knit me together in my mother's womb.

87

> I thank you for the wonder of my being,
> for the wonders of all your creation.
> Already you knew my soul,
> my body held no secret from you
> when I was being fashioned in secret
> and moulded in the depths of the earth.
> (Ps. 139 (138).13–15, Grail)

Out of chaos, out of the formless, lifeless darkness, God brought the world for us, and us for himself.

During the centuries after the exile, speculation and meditation on the creative work of God was taken further by the sages who continued an ancient tradition of popular wisdom but gave it an emphasis proper to their own faith. In poems of great beauty Wisdom was personified.[3] Wisdom is a female figure, who has been with God from eternity and shares his divine attributes, yet is in some way distinct from him. She was present as a collaborator in his creative work:

> When there was yet no ocean I was born,
> no springs brimming with water.
> Before the mountains were settled in their place,
> long before the hills I was born,
> when as yet he had made neither land nor lake
> nor the first clod of earth.
> When he set the heavens in their place I was there,
> when he girdled the ocean with the horizon,
> when he fixed the canopy of clouds overhead
> and set the springs of ocean firm in their place,
> when he prescribed its limits for the sea
> and knit together earth's foundations.
> Then I was at his side each day,
> his darling and delight,
> playing in his presence continually,
> playing on the earth, when he had finished it,
> while my delight was in mankind.
> (Prov. 8.24–31, NEB)

Wisdom at play in this passage recalls the 'Miraculous Child' of the myths.

She searched for a resting place among men, until at last the divine choice of Israel put an end to her nomadic wandering:

> Then the Creator of all things gave me a commandment,
> and the one who created me assigned a place for my tent.
> And he said, 'Make your dwelling in Jacob,
> and in Israel receive your inheritance'.
> (Sir. 24.8)

Fellowship with her brings benefits to human beings, for she is the source of wise counsel, virtuous living and discernment in all their affairs; she is more profitable to them than riches, and she wins them God's favour. Typical of these poems is Wisdom's invitation, 'Come', especially to share a feast she has prepared:

> Come, eat of my bread
> and drink of the wine I have mixed.
> (Prov. 9.5)

> Come to me, you who desire me,
> and eat your fill of my produce.
> For the remembrance of me is sweeter than honey,
> and my inheritance sweeter than the honeycomb.
> Those who eat me will hunger for more,
> and those who drink me will thirst for more.
> (Sir. 24.19–21)

The summit of this vivid personification of Wisdom was reached in the last century before Christ, in the Wisdom of Solomon. Wisdom is now unambiguously divine: in her is a spirit that is 'holy, all-powerful':

> She is a breath of the power of God,
> and a pure emanation of the glory of the Almighty;
> therefore nothing defiled gains entrance into her.
> For she is a reflection of eternal light,
> a spotless mirror of the working of God,
> and an image of his goodness.
> (Wisd. 7.25–6)

Yet holy, pure and elevated as she is, she is not remote, for

> Wisdom is more mobile than any motion;
> because of her pureness she pervades and penetrates all
>   things. . . .
> While remaining in herself she renews all things;
> in every generation she passes into holy souls
> and makes them friends of God, and prophets.
> (Wisd. 7.24, 27)

Here we are at the heart of the matter. Never had the concept of God's Wisdom been so high, yet never had the intimacy of his immanent presence to all that he has made been affirmed with such certainty. For various pagan religious philosophies, especially those of the Gnostics during the centuries immediately before and after the coming of Christ, there was irreconcilable opposition between the holiness of God and matter. The transcendent God must be protected from defiling contact with the material world by chains of intermediaries; indeed, he cannot even directly have created it. Israel never fell into this mistake. However high, holy and transcendent their God, contact with his creatures was never thought to compromise him. He is at home in his universe. The poems on personified divine Wisdom, like the passages where Yahweh's Word seems almost a personal being distinct from him, are a striking assertion not only of his creative activity in some remote past but of his constant indwelling in all he has made and his desire to communicate with his creatures. Wisdom, like the Word, is a communication and a means of friendship between God and men. She is 'an *outpouring* of God's glory'. She is at play in the world continually, finding her delight in mankind; she is for ever 'passing into holy souls and making them friends of God and prophets'. She plays, she dances, she reveals; she is powerful and tender; she stands for exchange and beauty, for life that is given and received.

These intuitions do not suggest that Israelites of the Old Testament period believed in a God of three Persons. The time for that revelation had not yet come, and rocklike faith in the unique, undivided God of Israel was its indispensable condition. The reconciliation of Jewish monotheism with full trinitarian faith took time, and was probably not complete until near the end of the New Testament period. Nevertheless, the Old Testament's personification of Wisdom and the Word was more than a poetic device. Divine perfection was understood to be not remoteness but the will to communicate. God is infinitely near his work, present at the heart and core of his creatures' life, not defiled or lowered by contact with them. His holiness is not solitude but self-giving; he wants to share himself, and that is his glory. Minds were being oriented towards the truth which could be revealed only through the sending of the Son and the gift of the Spirit: God is so much that kind of God that outpouring of self between divine Persons is constitutive of his very being.

About fifty years before the incarnation, a prayer was written into the Wisdom of Solomon in which the inspired author finally begged God to *send* his Wisdom:

> God of our ancestors, Lord of mercy,
> who by your word have made all things,
> and in your wisdom have fitted man
> to rule the creatures that have come from you. . . .
> With you is Wisdom, she who knows your works,
> she who was present when you made the world;
> she understands what is pleasing in your eyes
> and what agrees with your commandments.
> Despatch her from the holy heavens,
> send her forth from your throne of glory
> to help me and to toil with me
> and teach me what is pleasing to you,
> since she knows and understands everything.
> She will guide me prudently in my undertakings
> and protect me by her glory.
> (Wisd. 9.1–2, 9–11, JB)

An *inspired* prayer is asking God to send that incarnate Wisdom who in the person of Jesus Christ will be born two or three generations later. God inspires in us the longings he himself intends to fulfil, so that two loves may meet, ours and his.

The serene optimism of the Wisdom hymns and the beauty of the two creation accounts in Genesis are not the Old Testament's whole view of creation, for close upon the latter comes the story of how God's handiwork is smashed. Sin gets in, and the harmony is broken. Man is at odds with God, with his fellow humans, and with the earth and its animal population. When sin reaches a certain level, the floodgates God carefully provided break down, and water engulfs nearly everything. Chaos has come back. There is mercy, and a remnant is preserved to make a new, clean start; but chaos is always there, held back, but threatening whenever man's wickedness accumulates.

There are different manifestations of chaos in Scripture. The lifeless void awaited God's creative act in the beginning. The wilderness of the exodus was a historical manifestation of chaos, a place unsown, lifeless, without order, like the chaotic, barren darkness of the beginning. That time of displacement was remembered by later Israel as a period of empty dread, like an experience of the primordial chaos. In the time of the prophets the sin-ridden nation, corrupt and spiritually sick, appeared to Jeremiah like chaos returned:

> I looked on the earth, and lo, it was waste and void;
> and to the heavens, and they had no light.
> I looked on the mountains, and lo, they were quaking,
> and all the hills moved to and fro.
> I looked, and lo, there was no man,
> and all the birds of the air had fled.
> I looked, and lo, the fruitful land was a desert,
> and all its cities were laid in ruins
> before the Lord, before his fierce anger.
> (Jer. 4.23-6)

The destruction soon to be wrought by the Babylonian invader was only a ratification of what sin had already done in Israel, a visible, external manifestation of the chaos in Israelite hearts. The situation was therefore hopeless, because a sinful people was impotent to change itself. Jeremiah saw this clearly. Nothing less than a creative act of God would be needed, but this is exactly what he and Ezekiel predicted. At the centre of their prophecies is the promise of a new covenant between the Lord and Israel, and it is to be made possible by the creation of a new heart in man:

> A new heart I will give you, and a new spirit I will put within you; and I will take out of your flesh the heart of stone and give you a heart of flesh.
> (Ezek. 36.26)

A psalmist, perhaps influenced by these prophecies, prayed for the gift in what has become a classic expression of repentance and of man's inability to change his own deep heart:

> O purify me, then I shall be clean;
> O wash me, I shall be whiter than snow. . . .
> From my sins turn away your face
> and blot out all my guilt.
> A pure heart *create* for me, O God.[4]

It may have been just after this, during the chaos of the exile, that the priestly history, of which Genesis 1 is the opening and part of the flood story a continuation, took its final form. It is a heroic act of faith: our God is the Lord of chaos, who can push back empires now, as once he pushed back waters, and bring his people once more to firm, dry ground. His word can call forth light, order, life, fruitfulness and a history out of what is formless, hopeless and void.[5]

During Holy Week, when the Church celebrates Christ's passion, the liturgy for many centuries used the Book of Lamentations. These elegiac poems mourn directly over ravaged, desolate Jerusalem, laid waste by the invading Babylonian army. But Jerusalem so ravaged and reduced to chaos was only the outward sign of the people's sin, as Jeremiah had seen. At another level the ruined, chaotic city is a sign of Jesus, broken and torn and 'made sin for us', and of ourselves in our sin and helplessness.

Into the dark negativity of the chaotic waters Jesus descended in his passion. His baptism in the Jordan had already been a prophetic sign of this, as his emergence from the Jordan to hear the Father's word of love and receive the

Spirit had been a sign of his resurrection. The passion is the hour of darkness and inrushing chaos:

> Save me, O God,
> for the waters have risen to my neck.
> I have sunk into the mud of the deep
> and there is no foothold.
> I have entered the waters of the deep
> and the waves overwhelm me. . . .
> Do not let the deep engulf me
> nor death close its mouth on me.
> (Ps. 69 (68).2, 3, 16, Grail)

Jesus, the self-emptying Servant, is the Word in whom and through whom all things were made, the Wisdom of God who played delightedly before him in creation. He is identified now with the ruined cosmos, with ruined man who has dragged it down with himself, and with us in our chaos and emptiness. But in him torn creation, reduced to chaos, is once more obedient to God. In his passion and resurrection the new creation is wrought. The great week of it echoes the week of the beginnings: on the sixth day, recalling the sixth day of Genesis when man was created, Jesus dies. On the seventh day, the day of God's rest in Genesis, Jesus rests after the great battle. On the eighth day, Sunday, the beginning of the new week, the new time of the new creation opens in a new garden. These events have stamped our Christian rhythm of the week since apostolic times.

Jesus was not saved from the deep, chaotic waters of death, but by going down into them in obedient love he changed their meaning. They became the womb of the new creation, the birthplace of a cosmos to be re-created in him. As St Gregory Nazianzen says of Christ's baptism, 'When Jesus came up from the waters, he raised up with him a whole sunken world'.[6]

Jesus Christ is the Lord of chaos, so on Easter evening he comes to his disciples and breathes on them. Over the old chaos of sin hovers the Spirit – the Breath – of the Word, the risen and glorified Word made flesh: 'Receive the Holy

FIRST-BORN OF ALL CREATION

Spirit. If you forgive the sins of any, they are forgiven' (John 20.23). They rejoice, he rejoices, God rejoices in what he has done, for behold, it is very good. Their joy no one can take from them. Man is lifted into the creative joy of God.[7]

The prologue of John's Gospel opens with the solemn phrase, 'In the beginning', which to any ear attuned to the Old Testament evokes the opening of Genesis. The echoes are already awakened, and John goes on to speak of the divine Word who has been made flesh in Jesus by using the pattern of the Wisdom hymns. Like Wisdom, the Word was with God in the beginning, and now it is plainly said that 'the Word was God'. With God, and yet God – the paradox seems impossible, unstatable. Certainly it is mystery, which no statement can reduce, but the Wisdom developments of the Old Testament provided some way of formulating the reality of Christ. Through the Word-Wisdom of the Father all things were created; he is the source of light and life for men, and he was 'in the world' even before his definitive coming as man. He was 'made flesh' and has become for us the revealer of the Father's glory, the communication of God's thought and wisdom, and the giver of the gift of sonship by which we share God's life. Later in John's first chapter Jesus goes about seeking disciples, like Wisdom who took her stand 'at the cross-roads, by the wayside', calling to men (cf. Prov. 8.1–21). Uncertainly, hopefully, the first disciples follow, seeking something to which they can hardly put a name: 'Rabbi, where are you staying?' And he answers, 'Come and see.' It is a natural, friendly reply that need have meant no more than it obviously says, but John has already told us that the Word is with God from all eternity, and that he is the only-begotten Son who is 'nearest to the Father's heart'. There is the place of his eternal 'abiding', and the invitation to those disciples and all his disciples is to 'come and see' much more than his earthly lodging.

The 'Come' note is struck again in John's sixth chapter, after the feeding of the five thousand in the wilderness. Jesus who is Word-Wisdom speaks of the banquet to which he invites all men: 'I am the bread of life; he who comes to me shall not hunger, and he who believes in me shall never thirst' (John 6.35).

Finally, in the prayer given by John at the end of the Last Discourse, Jesus who is Word and Wisdom speaks of the glory he had with the Father before the world was made. He has come forth from the Father as revealer, as the giver of God's life to men, and now he is to return, like the efficacious Word who will not return 'empty', but only after accomplishing all the Father's purpose (cf. Isa. 55.11).

Paul too drew on the Wisdom tradition in his struggle to express the reality of Christ, but used it in a different way. Confronted with the self-important and thoroughly frivolous 'wisdom' of the Corinthians he hammered home the paradoxes of the message he preached and the unlikely means God had chosen to propagate it. Christ had sent him

> to preach the gospel, and not with eloquent wisdom, lest the cross of Christ be emptied of its power. For the word of the cross is folly to those who are perishing, but to us who are being saved it is the power of God. . . . For Jews demand signs and Greeks seek wisdom, but we preach Christ crucified, a stumbling block to Jews and folly to Gentiles, but to those who are called, both Jews and Greeks, Christ the power of God and the wisdom of God. For the foolishness of God is wiser than men, and the weakness of God is stronger than men.
> (1 Cor. 1.17–18, 22–5)

More explicitly even than John, Paul saw Christ's redemptive work as a new creation. The splendour of the new covenant established in Christ outshines both the glory that radiated from the face of Moses after converse with Yahweh and the primordial light of the first creation, for 'it is the God who said, "Let light shine out of darkness," who has shone in our hearts to give the light of the knowledge of the glory of God in the face of Christ' (2 Cor. 4.6). The first man was created in God's image and likeness, but he defaced the divine image through sin. Christ is the image of the invisible God, and as we contemplate the glory in his face we regain the likeness we lost; we 'are being changed into his likeness from one degree of glory to another; for this comes from the Lord who is the Spirit' (2 Cor. 3.18).

This transformation of man is the re-creative act of God to which Jeremiah and Ezekiel pointed, but it goes further than they foresaw. Each of us is re-created not as a lone individual but as a member of the one 'new man', who is Christ. He is the new Adam, according to Paul, the head of the new race, and in his resurrection the new creation is inaugurated. The risen Christ is the pledge, promise and first-fruits of all new-born humanity, the radiant nucleus of a cosmos groaning in travail towards its own new birth. In his Letter to the Colossians Paul sees the primal creation and the resurrection in one single perspective, unified in Christ, who is both 'first-born of all creation' and 'first-born from the dead':

> He is the image of the unseen God, the first-born of all creation; for in him all things were created, in heaven and on earth, visible and invisible . . . all things were created through him and for him. He is before all things, and in him all things hold together. He is the head of the body, the Church; he is the beginning, the first-born from the dead, that in everything he might be pre-eminent.[8]

We are the new creation in Christ, but we still have a stake in the old chaos. We know something, from time to time, of the unloving, lifeless, impotent areas in ourselves. These, precisely, are to be yielded to the creative act of the God who brings life from death, not hidden or swept out of the way before we can pray to him. When you know yourself to be empty and poor and sterile, unable to love and live, when you experience in yourself the impossibility of giving life to others or of forgiving others as God forgives you, then you really know yourself to be the lifeless chaos. You are like the broken body of Jesus in the tomb, impotent to help yourself, awaiting the word of resurrection. Even the yielding of the chaos to him may be something you cannot actively do. But he is Lord of your chaos. Christ's descent into hell, into the depths of the earth, into the darkest depths of our sin and sterility, has given him the right to claim the domain of death as his own.

We have to pray from a position of chaos, because that is where we are, and that is the material on which the Spirit delights to work. The implications of this for personal prayer will be suggested in a moment, but it is worth noting first that the psalms can make great sense as chaotic prayer. They are full of darkness and conflict as well as joy in God's presence; they are not always pure praise but often ugly with vengeance, hatred and smugness. In the psalms people cry out in joy and pain, bewilderment and wonder, fear, shame and rebellion; and they go on tediously telling God about their tedious lives. This is the human condition as familiar to us. The psalms are about human experience, and no part of it is hidden from God or felt to be unmentionable in his presence. They were waiting for Christ, waiting to be taken up and transformed by him, waiting to be Christified, like all human experience. They were the raw material of his prayer, as the flesh of Israel was the raw material that would make his body, the stuff of his sacrifice. They were like unconsecrated hosts, destined for a fulfilment beyond themselves. His cry from the cross in the words of a psalm, 'My God, my God, why have you forsaken me?' gathered up all the inarticulate, chaotic cries of the poor and sinful in every generation of the world's history, and the cries of our own lives. Much in us is still pre-Christian and waits to be gathered into Christ's Easter.

Prayer is a listening to the creative, life-giving word that loves us into being. Yet prayer of a simple, contemplative kind, in which we try to stand before God and let him know us, not much preoccupied with particular thoughts but just loving, invariably produces a sense of our own sinfulness. There seem to be two distinct kinds of sin. One is a deliberate 'No' to God in any area whatever; this automatically cancels the simple kind of prayer, until it is repented of and a 'Yes' substituted. It is obvious why this must be so: life and prayer cannot be compartmentalized. The other kind of sinfulness makes itself felt in a global sense of being weak and shabby and in need of God's mercy, an awareness of the general slum-situation within. This kind is not an act but a state, and it almost seems to help; or at least the experience of it is part of prayer. You know that you are an undeserving beggar, that you have not a leg to stand on; yet somehow it is good to be there, because it is real, and to avoid this confrontation would be to escape into untruth. The strange thing is that although prayer is often completely unsatisfying and very humbling, although you seem to fail and fail again in prayer, you dimly know that it is all-important to stay there in that emptiness, refusing to fill the void with anything that is not God.

If this is your experience, you have attained to fellowship with the tax-collector in the Gospel. He had no achievements and no claim; he could only pray from his chaos, 'O God, be merciful to me, a sinner' (cf. Luke 18.13). All he could do was to make a space for God to be merciful, for God to be God for him. You have to make a space for God to be God for you, so that he can draw you into that truth-relationship with himself. This means space in the practical sense: you need a measure of time and silence to let him do it. It also means space in the sense of personal emptiness, not clinging to any righteousness of your own, letting go of any kind of inner defence against the living God. Then just abide there under his judgement and let him love you. He is a God who delights to give himself where there is hunger and thirst of spirit.

There are times in our lives when we are led deeply into the experience of inner poverty. You know that you have no prayer, no feeling of love or power to care, no words to speak when it is your duty to speak, nothing to give. Why does it happen? The obvious answer is, Because we have sinned. Certainly this is true; were it not, the experience would not be one of genuine personal poverty, but would be something that remained outside our real life with God, something that did not bite deeply. Nevertheless, God means it to happen; he does lead us into it, because he wants to open us wider to the reality of his salvation. Joseph was told, 'You shall call his name Jesus, for he will save his people from their sins' (Matt. 1.21). Until you know him as Jesus for you, you scarcely know him at all.

Repentance is an attitude of continual conversion of heart, and it is a poverty, because it means always beginning again, never being able to rely on past successes or attained positions after the manner of the rich, but always admitting your need of God's mercy. The need seems to grow greater as the years pass. Conversion is the fruit of grace, not the condition for grace to be offered. We do not somehow make ourselves respectable at a distance, and then approach God in prayer. Conversion is much more than our own good resolution to turn over a new leaf; it means going down into the dark chaotic waters and allowing ourselves to be re-created by God's act, not once but many times.

In Christ, the first-born of all creation, in Christ, the Word through whom all things were made, God is creating you *now*. He is breathing his creative Spirit upon your chaos, and speaking his word, 'Let there be you', *now*, not only once upon a time a few years ago when he loved you into existence. His creative love bears upon you today, with all the reality of God; it bears upon you in every dimension of your body and spirit. Every movement of your understanding, every movement of your heart, is directly his creation in you – his, but therefore truly and fully yours because he creates you and gives you to yourself. He is creating your mind, that marvellous and astonishing thing, as you read; he is creating in you the faith that seeks understanding. What does this mean when you reach out to someone in love or compassion or friendship? All that is good and loving, generous and spontaneous in you is his gift of the very moment, a direct, fresh, new gift, but really your own. What does it mean when you are before him trying to pray? Your whole being is his word of love; your faith is the dark knowing he creates in you so that you may reach out and touch him surely; your ability to listen is a power he is creating in you now, precisely because he wants you to hear the word of love he wants to speak.

We foolishly suppose that prayer is about our own efforts, our longing for God, our attempts to love and praise and thank him. But all this is only a consequence, a created response. Our prayer is God's work, God's creation. As you kneel there, sit there, walk about or whatever you do when you pray, you are saying 'Yes' with your whole being to his will that you should be, that you should be you, that you should be united to him. Your prayer is God's word of longing and love in you, God's breathing of the Spirit in you, to make you want the union he wants. His desire is going through your heart to leap up to him and meet his desire again, like the desire of that writer who prayed to God to 'send Wisdom'; yet it is truly your desire because he creates it as yours. His love is loving through your heart when you try to pray. You are tuning in to, consenting to, something that is real anyway, whether you know it or not:

> for we do not know how to pray as we ought, but the Spirit himself intercedes for us with sighs too deep for words. And he who searches the hearts of men knows what is the mind of the Spirit, because the Spirit intercedes for the saints according to the will of God.
> (Rom. 8.26–7)

When Christ came to his disciples at Easter as the Lord of the new creation, breathing the re-creative Spirit upon them, he came as the one who is so identified with us that even as he breathes the Spirit he bears upon his body the chaotic signs, the wounds in hands and feet and side which are the marks of the chaos we made, the chaos we are. They are transfigured wounds, not the wounds of the Friday. But they are not simply effaced; he keeps them as tokens of re-creative love, transfigured.

His faithfulness to us in that union means that the Father cannot look upon us, in our woundedness and brokenness, apart from Christ. Our wounds are not simply effaced, either; in him they are healed and transfigured, and become tokens of love. His healing love is at work in you, and needs your answering love and consent so that it may flow through you to other broken and wounded human beings.

Your prayer, your chaos-marked efforts to pray, are part of God's new creation, part of the Spirit's glorious, re-creative act in Christ, in the renewed cosmos. In it he rejoices, and you must too, however chaotic it may still appear to you. You have to consent to being loved by an optimistic God who considers that creation is a success, and joyfully keeps on uttering his creative word. You have better reason than the psalmist to say,

> I thank you for the wonder of my being,
> for the wonders of all your creation.
> (Ps. 139 (138).14, Grail)

There is wisdom and delight for us in the marvels of our new creation. It is not all hidden from us, because God cannot wait to tell us:

> The Spirit explores everything, even the depths of God's own nature. . . . Only the Spirit of God knows what God is. This is the Spirit that we have received from God . . . so that we may know all that God of his own grace has given us.
> (1 Cor. 2.10–12, NEB)

Wisdom dances and plays in the new creation, 'penetrating all things', breaking down the barriers which sealed off person from person, sense from spirit, earth from heaven and time from eternity. There is exchange, giving and receiving, and the healing of our senses even now. We are invited to join in the dance, and in so doing we join in the creativity.

Obedient creativity is very demanding. Because I am in the dance, because the dance is the life of the Trinity flowing through creation, I receive only to give, and in giving I receive again and the more there is to give. If I have listened to the word I may also be asked to speak it, and I cannot be selective in the speaking any more than in the listening, though there is the endless search to know and understand what speaking is demanded by the delicacy of love. And here again there is a poverty at the heart of things, because the creative act that has been beautiful and blessed cannot be repeated. It was a unique beauty and I cannot cling to it lest I degrade it; I must give it away and go on living, and try to be open to the new thing that the Lord God will do.

On the brink of the new venture, the little new creation that will pass through me, demanding my all, I tremble, so much wanting it to be beautiful, yet aware of the gap between dream and embodiment. Then perhaps I am with the prophets who heard a new call, with Mary just pregnant and wanting the child to be glorious but not for herself, with Jesus as he heard the new word, 'I love you', at his baptism and set out on the mighty work, the great risk, the beautiful enterprise that would be glorious only through his own dying.

Jesus is the Holy One and I am sinful, yet the comparison is not invalid for that. Isaiah cried out that he was unclean and the Lord cleansed his lips with the holy fire; so also he can cleanse me with the fire of his Spirit if he entrusts his word and work to me, so that it will go through me as his word of power and love. I cannot fit myself for work any more than for prayer, nor can I seek his will in the doing as though I had to keep applying for instructions to someone outside myself. It is much closer than that. His springing creativity is in me at the core of my being: his love, his truth, his desire to give himself, his surging life and his will that creation should go on. My chaotic inadequacy does not deter him.

7 Glory Reinterpreted

Thus shall the glory of the Lord be revealed,
and all mankind together shall see it;
for the Lord himself has spoken. . . .
Arise, Jerusalem,
rise clothed in light; your light has come
and the glory of the Lord shines over you.
> Isaiah 40.5; 60.1, NEB

Jerusalem is the Holy City for three of the great faiths of the world, and it has been a symbol of hope and promise in the lives of countless human beings for about three millennia. For a thousand years before Christ's coming, Jerusalem was Yahweh's chosen dwelling. It represented his whole people, and its fortunes reflected their relationship with him. In the fullness of time Israel's Messiah came to Jerusalem, taught and healed there, and was judged, cast out and crucified. There he rose from the dead, there he sent his Spirit upon the Easter community, and from Jerusalem the gospel spread outwards to the world.

Jerusalem means first of all a real earthly city with a long history, still seething with life today. It is also a symbol of the Church on earth, which is God's dwelling-place among men and a visible sign of his grace. In the New Testament it stands for the glorified Church in heaven, the whole redeemed people, the Bride of the Lamb. Finally Jerusalem can mean every believer who through grace is the dwelling-place and the beloved of God. During Advent the liturgy plays in poetry and song on this archetypal city, but the rich symbolism is earthed in experience, because all the history of salvation is focused here.

The Israelite tribes who invaded the promised land under Joshua's leadership in about 1200 BC did not immediately oust the previous tenants; strong pockets of Canaanite resistance remained for generations. Jerusalem, a natural stronghold, was held by the Jebusites, and fell into Israelite hands only in David's time, some 200 years later. David was shrewd enough to make it his capital, realizing that it was not only an easy place to defend, but also a 'neutral' city associated with neither northern nor southern Israelite tribes. To Zion he brought the Ark of the Covenant, the visible symbol of Yahweh's desert-dwelling amid his people. From that moment onwards there was an indissoluble association in their minds between king, holy city and God.

The magnificent temple built by Solomon became the Lord's dwelling, where he promised to be present to his people's prayers when they 'sought his face'. Above the Ark his abiding glory dwelt among them. Jerusalem became the pride and joy of pilgrims. Within its walls flowed the quiet waters of Shiloah, symbol of the Lord's silent protection. Jerusalem was Yahweh's bride, called to be the faithful city, but prophet after prophet denounced its sins as harlotry. Terrible chastisement overtook it in the early sixth century:

> All those who pass by
> snap their fingers at you;
> they hiss and wag their heads at you,
> daughter of Jerusalem:
> 'Is this the city once called Perfect in beauty,
> Joy of the whole earth?'
> (Lam. 2.15, NEB)

By the waters of Babylon the exiles wept, remembering Zion, but the restoration of the holy city was central in the glowing promises made to them by Second Isaiah:

> Comfort, comfort my people,
> says your God.
> Speak tenderly to Jerusalem,
> and say to her
> that her warfare is ended,
> that her inquity is pardoned,
> that she has received from the Lord's hand
> double for all her sins.
> (Isa 40.1-2)

105

Jerusalem, forgiven and rehabilitated, will be taken back; there has been no divorce. She is to be mother of the nations, the rallying-point for all the Gentiles who will seek the Lord. In her God's covenant of peace with all mankind will be honoured. A response used during Advent evokes it:

> Return, O virgin Israel, return to these your cities. How long will you waver? You shall bring forth the Lord your Saviour, a new offering on the earth; men shall walk in the paths of salvation.

As the nations stream towards it the new Jerusalem is to be alight with God's glory:

> For behold, darkness shall cover the earth,
> and thick darkness the peoples;
> but the Lord will arise upon you,
> and his glory will be seen upon you.
> And nations shall come to your light,
> and kings to the brightness of your rising.
> (Isa. 60.2-3)

The 'glory' of the Lord was originally thought of as a visible, splendid light shed by his presence; in the desert the cloud which signified his presence was accompanied by fire. The fiery glory covered Mount Sinai at the time when Yahweh made his covenant with Israel, and some of it remained glowing from Moses's face when he returned to the people after converse with the Lord. An idea of 'weightiness' also clung to the meaning of 'glory', and at least from the eighth century BC the notion of moral perfection was associated with it. In the great vision of Isaiah of Jerusalem the fire is present, but the seer's immediate reaction is horror at his own impurity before the holiness of God:

> Above him stood the seraphim [i.e. 'the burning ones']
> . . . One called to another and said:
>   'Holy, holy, holy is the Lord of hosts;
>   the whole earth is full of his glory.'. . .
> And I said: 'Woe is me! For I am lost; for I am a man of unclean lips, and I dwell in the midst of a people of unclean

> lips; for my eyes have seen the King, the Lord of hosts!'
> Then flew one of the seraphim to me, having in his hand a
> burning coal. . . . And he touched my mouth, and said:
> 'Behold, this has touched your lips; your guilt is taken
> away, and your sins forgiven.'
> (Isa. 6.2-3,5-7)

Parallel to the manifestation of Yahweh's glory by dazzling radiance was another: the revelation of his glory by his mighty acts. The crossing of the sea and the drowning of Pharaoh's army won him glory (cf. Exod. 14.18), and the miracle of manna in the desert was an occasion on which Israel saw the glory of the Lord (cf. Exod. 16.10). This brought the idea of glory very close to the experience of salvation; Yahweh manifested his glory in a special way by his saving interventions, by putting his power, love and faithfulness at the service of his covenant-people. His glory was dynamic as well as radiantly beautiful. Both aspects were part of his reality, and the Old Testament's idea of glory has been summed up as 'holiness with the lid off'.

The glory was expected to rub off on to his people, but not always in the mystical and moral senses perceived by Moses and Isaiah. It was all too easy to distort Israel's vocation as a universal sign of salvation and a cynosure for the Gentiles into a claim to privilege and power. Glory for Israel could be interpreted in terms of wealth and success, victory, domination and the crushing of enemies. Under David and Solomon this was mostly what it had meant. Nevertheless, in Second Isaiah's prophecies the radiant beauty of Jerusalem is clearly to be the consequence of Yahweh's reign there and the city's own moral purification, and in some post-exilic writers the same spiritual awareness of Jerusalem's true glory is evident. Of particular beauty is a prophecy from the late sixth century BC:

> Jerusalem is to remain unwalled, because of the great
> number of men and cattle there will be in her. But I – it is
> Yahweh who speaks – I will be a wall of fire for her all round
> her, and I will be her glory in the midst of her.
> (Zech. 2.4-5, JB)

The walls were in fact rebuilt later, but the vision speaks of openness, of the giving and exchange of life. The messianic Jerusalem was to need no powerful protection and no glory other than the Lord himself.

In St Luke's Gospel Jerusalem is pivotal. His Infancy Narrative moves towards a climax in the presentation of the child in the temple, where Malachi's prophecy is fulfilled and Simeon acclaims the child who is both the glorious answer to Israel's hopes and the light-bearer to the Gentiles. The only subsequent episode in Luke's first two chapters is the loss and finding of Jesus at twelve years old; here again the scene is Jerusalem and the temple, and, as we have seen, the story has paschal overtones. Luke later recounts a large part of Jesus's public life in the form of a travel story: in Chapter 9, after the Transfiguration and the second prediction of the passion, Jesus 'sets his face to go to Jerusalem', and the material of the next ten chapters is presented as part of what happens on the way. The scheme is obviously artificial but focuses attention on Jerusalem, the place of God's salvation. Jesus finally reaches the holy city, and weeps over its faithlessness and impending tragedy. An earlier word in Luke's Gospel brings out the poignancy even more sharply:

> O Jerusalem, Jerusalem, killing the prophets and stoning those who are sent to you! How often would I have gathered your children together as a hen gathers her brood under her wings, and you would not!
> (Luke 13.34)

Jesus's feelings about Jerusalem must have been intense and ambivalent. When he 'set his face' to go there he knew he was courting hostility, danger and probably death. It would have been much easier to stay in Galilee where people were simpler and he was generally well received, and there is a kind of bitter irony in his words, 'It cannot be that a prophet should perish away from Jerusalem' (Luke 13.33). Yet Jerusalem was also the beloved city, and he resonated to all that it meant for a Jew: all the memories, all the vividly remembered thousand years of Israel's holiest place. The patriotism that was strong in him was bound up with his love and reverence for the God of Israel who had chosen this city; he loved Jerusalem and he ached for it. He knew the prophets' visions of a beautiful, purified, radiant Jerusalem alight with the glory of God. He relived with even more intensity the tearing of heart that had been the lot of Jeremiah, passionately in love with Jerusalem but sent to preach its doom and destruction. Jerusalem was to reject Jesus and he was to be crucified 'outside the camp' (cf. Heb. 13.12-13), but he was mystically identified with it and could not ultimately reject it any more than could the God who had grieved over his unfaithful people:

> How can I give you up! . . .
> How can I hand you over, O Israel! . . .
> My heart recoils within me,
> my compassion grows warm and tender.
> I will not execute my fierce anger . . .
> for I am God and not man,
> the Holy One in your midst,
> and I will not come to destroy.
> (Hos. 11.8-9)

Above all, Jerusalem was the place of his destiny, the place where his Father willed him to go. There he would know the Father and be known by him, in that intimacy to which the maturity of his obedient love would lay him open. That was the pull.

Anyone who faithfully prays knows this same mixture of desire and dread. We want God; we long for union with him, holiness and perfect love. We want to be entirely given. We lift our eyes to the hills, to the vision of the heights, to Jerusalem, the mountain city called Vision of Peace. Yet we fear the pain, the dying, the surrender, the losing of self, the ultimate letting-go. There may seem to be good reasons for not going (whether the 'going' that is being asked includes some outward step or not): there is work we can do for the Lord without *that*; indeed, to go may spell the end of our usefulness. At the same time we know that this one thing is being asked and we cannot evade it, at any rate not for long, and that anything else we may be doing will lose its meaning if we refuse that call. Union with God in unqualified surrender is our Jerusalem, the beloved city, the place of our destiny, and it draws us. It is supremely attractive, even though we know it means suffering and humiliation, and so there is joy amid the dread. Only there can we know the Father and be known by him; suffering is the place where this mutual knowledge can become perfect. We know God even as we suffer, and we know him in a different way afterwards as we look back on it. The Entrance Song on Easter Sunday in the Roman Missal adapts Psalm 139 (138): Jesus is speaking to his Father: 'I am risen and am still with you . . . . You laid your hand upon me. . . wonderful is your knowledge of me.'

If we experience this blend of love and shrinking we are not alone; Jesus knew it too. We are like the disciples in Mark's vivid picture:

> They were on the road, going up to Jerusalem, and Jesus was walking ahead of them; and they were amazed and those who followed were afraid.
> (Mark 10.32)

But they continued to follow him. Glory was coming to Jerusalem, despite itself.

Some 580 years earlier, at the time of the exile, Second Isaiah's Book of Consolation had been full of joyful reassurance. A restored Jerusalem would be radiant with God's glory. But amid the lyrical promises come the four poems distinguished by modern scholars as the Servant Songs.[1] Jerusalem had been told that the Lord would be its light and that the light would shine for the nations, but now it seemed that only through the Servant would this mission be fulfilled:

> Now the Lord says,
> who formed me from the womb to be his servant,
> to bring back Jacob to him,
> and that Israel might be gathered to him . . .
> 'It is too light a thing that you should be my servant

to raise up the tribes of Jacob . . .
I will give you as a light to the nations,
that my salvation may reach to the end of the earth.'
(Isa. 49.5-6)

Against the luminous background of the radiant promises to
Zion towers the sombre figure of the Servant with

no form or comeliness that we should look at him,
and no beauty that we should desire him.
He was despised and rejected by men;
a man of sorrows and acquainted with grief;
and as one from whom men hide their faces.
(Isa. 53.2-3)

There is indeed a perspective of glory in the Servant Songs,
and to this representative of the people, who is also more
than a representative, the Lord says, 'You are my servant,
Israel, in whom I will be glorified'.[2] But it becomes evident
that the glory in question is not the kind Israel expected.
God's promise of peace, vindication and a glorious future for
Jerusalem had often been taken to imply victory over its
oppressors, but according to the fourth song the Servant's
destiny is to become vulnerable to all that oppressors can do:

He was oppressed, and he was afflicted,
yet he opened not his mouth;
like a lamb that is led to the slaughter,
and like a sheep that before its shearers is dumb,
so he opened not his mouth.
By oppression and judgment he was taken away.
(Isa. 53.7-8)

He was innocent, yet he 'has borne our griefs and carried our
sorrows . . . and the Lord has laid on him the inquity of us
all' (Isa. 53.4,6). Numbered with criminals he yet 'bore the
sin of many, and made intercession for the transgressors'
(Isa. 53.12) and his self-offering became a sacrifice to expiate
the sins of many.

   In this Suffering Servant, whose fidelity to God brings him
to an unjust death, a death which is yet a redemptive

sacrifice, at least three lines of Israel's expectation intersect. The problem of why the innocent suffer had perplexed many minds and touched the lives of the *'anawim*; the priestly tradition had been preoccupied with the efficacy of sacrifice; the prophetic traditions had asserted that the intercession of a righteous man, particularly a prophet, could avail on behalf of a sinful people. This fourth Servant Song touched a height of spiritual insight never again reached in the Old Testament. It was one of those breakthroughs apparently not followed up; if we do not surrender ourselves to the grace we have and consent to live at the new level, we fall away from it again.

It may be, however, that in some Jewish circles similiar ideas and hopes were maintained, but found no single clear expression comparable to the Servant Songs. There were certainly hopes that a righteous prophet would come, who would be the 'anointed of the Lord' in a perhaps even more significant way than were the Davidic kings:

> The Spirit of the Lord God is upon me,
> because the Lord has anointed me
> to bring good tidings to the afflicted;
> he has sent me to bind up the brokenhearted.
> (Isa. 61.1)

In the Wisdom of Solomon another prophet-like figure appears, who enjoys unprecedented intimacy with God whom he calls his Father and in his innocence is hated by the wicked, suffers and dies, but is somehow vindicated after death. The godless complain:

> 'The virtuous man . . . claims to have knowledge of God,
> and calls himself a son of the Lord. . . .
> He holds aloof from our doings as though from filth;
> he proclaims the final end of the virtuous as happy
> and boasts of having God for his father.
> Let us see if what he says is true,
> let us observe what kind of end he himself will have.
> If the virtuous man is God's son, God will take his part
> and rescue him from the clutches of his enemies.

> Let us test him with cruelty and with torture,
> and thus explore this gentleness of his. . . .'
> (Wisd. 2.12,13,16-19, JB)

But eventually these godless oppressors

> will come trembling to the reckoning of their sins,
> and their crimes, confronting them, will accuse them.
> Then the virtuous man stands up boldly
> to face those who have oppressed him,
> those who thought so little of his sufferings.
> And they, at sight of him, will shake with cowards' fear,
> amazed he should be saved so unexpectedly.
> (Wisd. 4.20—5.2, JB)

If the kind of hopes expressed in Isaiah 61 and Wisdom 2 and 5 were current in the circles where Jesus moved, it is easier to explain his reinterpretation of 'Messiah' or 'Anointed One'. He moved it away from the warrior-prince idea of the Davidic tradition, seeing his own vocation more in terms of the suffering prophet who lives in intimacy with God his Father.[3]

Israel needed re-education in order to be 'a covenant for the nations'; to be, that is, the people caught up in the covenant-love of the God who was ultimately revealed in Jesus, and this for the sake of all humankind. They needed to learn how to see the glory of their vocation not in terms of status, power and privilege, but in service and, where necessary, suffering, in order that God's glory might shine through them for all. A parallel process of re-education was needed by the Twelve who were the foundation members of God's new Israel, and the middle part of St Mark's Gospel vividly depicts it. At the centre of the Gospel Jesus puts the crucial question, 'Who do you say I am?' (cf. Mark 8.29). What kind of master do you think you are following? What are your expectations? Peter answers rightly, in the name of them all: 'You are the Messiah.' So far, so good, but Jesus immediately redefines that term:

> He began to teach them that the Son of man must suffer many things, and be rejected by the elders and the chief

113

> priests and the scribes, and be killed, and after three days
> rise again.
> (Mark 8.31).

This first prediction of his passion is greeted with incomprehension, and Jesus spells out the conditions of discipleship: 'If any man would come after me, let him deny himself and take up his cross and follow me.' In the following chapter there is a second prediction of the passion in similar terms, 'but they did not understand the saying, and they were afraid to ask him' (Mark 9.32); how completely they have failed to understand is suggested by the episode that follows:

> They came to Capernaum; and . . . he asked them, 'What
> were you discussing on the way?' But they were silent; for
> on the way they had discussed with one another who was
> the greatest.
> (Mark 9.33-4)

They are still imprisoned within their own expectations of a kingdom of power. In Chapter 10 Jesus agains foretells his passion, and this time the immediate sequel as presented by Mark is the request made by James and John for the two top seats in the kingdom. This fresh evidence of incomprehension gives Jesus the opportunity to state clearly the real issue:

> You know that those who are supposed to rule over the
> Gentiles lord it over them, and their great men exercise
> authority over them. But it shall not be so among you; but
> whoever would be great among you must be your servant,
> and whoever would be first among you must be slave of all.
> For the Son of man also came not to be served but to serve,
> and to give his life as a ransom for many.[4]

This is an explicit claim to the Servant role as sketched in Isaiah 53. Luke puts a similar saying in the context of a dispute among the disciples at the Last Supper about who was the greatest: 'I am among you as one who serves' (Luke 22.27).

Whether the saying in Mark 10.42–5 quoted above goes

114

back in this form to Jesus himself, whether it was evoked by a request from James and John (Mark) or from their mother (Matthew) or by some more general argument about precedence among the apostles, whether such ambitions surfaced once or several times, it seems clear that we have here an echo of the slow re-educative process through which the first disciples learned that Jesus's messianic glory was to be understood in terms of service, suffering and self-sharing love. It took the passion and Easter to bring them to full understanding. Surely, however, we should think of the process as also in some way necessary to Jesus himself. In Chapter 5 of this book it was suggested that in his lifelong listening to the Father's word, in his grappling with the mystery of himself and his vocation, Jesus needed people. He needed the response and reaction of other minds to clarify his own; he needed his friends' understanding to understand himself. But surely their misunderstanding served him too. There are times when someone speaks to you, or a group of people are discussing something that deeply concerns you, and you find yourself reacting sharply: they have got it wrong; the whole approach is wrong. You may not be able to put your finger on the falsehood, but it is as plainly false as someone singing out of tune, and it jars. This experience may force you to think through the question more clearly than you have before, and to define for yourself where you stand. Perhaps Jesus too reacted intuitively and emotionally to conversations which he felt to be out of tune with his understanding of the Father, and was forced to make explicit what had previously been implicit and unfocused: his acceptance of his vocation to be the Servant of the Lord.

The most explicit identification of Jesus with the Servant is made by the First Letter of Peter:

> He committed no sin; no guile was found on his lips. When he was reviled, he did not revile in return; when he suffered, he did not threaten; but he trusted to him who judges justly. He himself bore our sins in his body on the

115

> tree, that we might die to sin and live to righteousness. By
> his wounds you have been healed. For you were straying
> like sheep . . . .
> (1 Pet. 2.22-5)

The same certainty, though in less explicitly allusive
language, underlies the hymn of Philippians 2.5-11, sometimes held to be an already existing hymn taken over by Paul.
Here the full theological sweep from divine pre-existence,
through human self-emptying and the obedience of the
cross, to the exaltation of Christ in glory, gives the Servant
mystery its fullest statement. Christ was 'in the form of God'
and divine glory was his by right, but he emptied himself
and took the condition of a servant. Humbly living and
humbly obedient even to the death of the cross, he was
highly exalted and has received the supreme name, 'Lord',
so that all creation may confess that 'Jesus Christ is Lord, to
the glory of God the Father'.

John treats this mystery in his own way, seldom directly
quoting the Servant prophecies but telling the story of Jesus
as a revelation of the glory. The Word was made flesh 'and
we have beheld his glory, glory as of the only Son from the
Father'.[5] The 'signs' round which the first half of John's
Gospel is built are manifestations of Jesus's glory, beginning
with the marriage feast at Cana and reaching a climax at the
raising of Lazarus: 'Have I not told you that if you believe you
will see the glory of God?' (John 11.40, JB). Throughout the
Gospel, John plays on the idea of 'exaltation' or 'lifting up',
alluding to the double sense of Jesus being raised up on the
cross and exalted in glory.

The final 'sign' is the whole complex of events through
which this supreme manifestation of glory is achieved. At
the Last Supper the glory of God is shown to be simply love:
the Father's love for the Son and the Son's love for the Father
in their common Spirit; the Father's love for the world and
especially for the disciples, manifested in the gift of his Son;
the Son's humble, serviceable love expressed in washing the
disciples' feet and laying down his life for them; and the
answering, participative love which binds the disciples to

Jesus and to one another. This is 'glory'. In his prayer after
the supper Jesus says to the Father, 'The glory which thou
hast given me I have given to them, that they may be one
even as we are one' (John 17.22).

Earlier in the Gospel John has reported Jesus's remark to
the Jews, 'I do not seek my own glory . . . . If I glorify
myself, my glory is nothing; it is my Father who glorifies
me'(John 8.50,54). The meaning of this is made clear by the
unfolding of events. Through Jesus's human unselfishness
and loving-unto-the-end God's glory is manifested, because
glory is divine unselfishness, self-sharing love. Jesus can be
revealed as fully 'glorious' only when he is broken; and only
when he is broken and so glorified can he give the Spirit,
because the Spirit is God's self-sharing love, God's glory.[6]

It was Paul, not John, who spoke of 'the glory of God in the
face of Christ' (2 Cor. 4.6), but John must have known it too,
and special to him is the emphasis on the revelation of glory
in the hour of the passion . If the traditional identification of
the John who stands behind the Fourth Gospel with the
beloved disciple at the foot of the cross is correct, he had
plenty of time to study that face. It was the Servant's face,
with 'no form or comeliness', bloody, bruised and sweating,
with the death pallor on it. But John had eyes to see, at least
in retrospect, that there the glory of the only-begotten was
revealed. He saw the same face after the resurrection, in the
upper room and across the water of the lake early in the
morning. Evidently it was not dazzling, as at the Transfiguration, but the glory was there to be seen by anyone with
faith and healed senses.

> The cross was the will of the Father, the glory of the Son,
> the joy of the Holy Spirit. It was the boast of Paul, who
> said: 'Let me boast of nothing except the cross of our Lord
> Jesus Christ.' The cross is brighter than the sun, its rays
> are more brilliant. When the sun is darkened the cross
> shines forth, for the darkness of the sun does not mean
> that it no longer exists, but that it is outshone by the
> splendour of the cross . . . . The cross is the proof of
> God's love, for 'God loved the world so much that he

gave his only Son to save those who believe in him from perishing'.[7]

The Word was made flesh and we saw his glory because he entered fully into our vulnerable situation, into the powerlessness of the oppressed, into our brokenness. This brokenness has become the place where the glorious, self-emptying love of the God who is Trinity has become operative within the human situation. Evil manifests itself by many forms of oppression, captivity and hatred, but because Christ has entered this sin-dominated situation, made all its brokenness his own and made that very condition the expression of forgiving, obedient, self-surrendering love, the meaning of the situation has changed. The conditions remain, but their significance is radically altered. Only in this way could oppression be overcome. Jesus has 'led captivity captive'.

A particular instance of this transformation by the love which expressed itself finally on the cross may be noted here, because it is linked to the motif of sterility and childlessness which were seen as aspects of personal poverty in Chapter 3. Jesus the Servant died alone, entrusting his life, his 'future', into the Father's hands. This is one aspect of his celibacy; in the Jewish way of thinking children were a person's primary insurance for the future, the surest way of prolonging one's own life. Jesus is wholly poor. Yet by his own new birth through death, through the narrow door to light, he gives birth to many:

> When he makes himself an offering for sin,
> he shall see his offspring, he shall prolong his days . . .
> he shall see the fruit of the travail of his soul and be satisfied;
> by his knowledge shall the righteous one, my servant,
> make many to be accounted righteous. . . .
> Therefore I will divide him a portion with the great,
> and he shall divide the spoil with the strong.
> (Isa. 53.10–12)

He is the new Adam, head of the new race, giver of life to the 'many'; he has given his flesh as 'bread for the life of the world', and his sacrifice is endlessly fruitful.

There was one person who through close association with Jesus had learnt the meaning of Israel's true glory, and that was the woman whom Luke presents as the Daughter of Zion, the woman of faith who was Israel as God meant it to be. Already in the Annunciation story there are hints of Easter. Mary's obedient 'Let it be done to me' foreshadows Jesus's 'Not as I will but as thou wilt'; the 'handmaid' (*doulē*) of Luke 1.38 is a counterpart to the Servant (*doulos*) of Philippians 2.7; Mary's 'lowliness' of which the Magnificat sings (*tapeinōsis*) is parallel to that of the Servant who 'humbled' (*etapeinōsen*) himself. This was only the beginning.

Anyone who reads the Gospels can guess what was the human anguish of the mother–son relationship as Mary stood by Jesus on Calvary, but it is important to remember also that she willed his sacrifice as truly as he did. In her measure she shared his consuming love for the Father's will, and made the offering with him, freely. This must have been of enormous significance to him as he held his will to it through agony and weakness; there was someone there who could be wholly one with him, supporting him in this most crucial decision of his life. In this hour too she was Israel – Israel bearing its Messiah in pain and consenting to die with him to all that was old and transitory, to make with him the passage to the Father. So the motherhood of Israel was accomplished in her. In the 'disciple whom Jesus loved' she accepted all the disciples whom Jesus loves, and became 'the mother of all the living'.[8]

The risen Jesus is transparent to the Father's glory, because as man, body and spirit, he belongs henceforth to the radiant sphere of God's holiness, beauty, power and life. But this divine glory which transforms him is self-sharing love, and the necessary fullness of his Easter mystery is its communication to all who are linked with him in the fellowship of his risen Body. In this communication, Jerusalem is again central. All the appearances of the risen Christ recorded by Luke, and all save one recorded by John,[9] take place in or near Jerusalem. According to Luke it is at Jerusalem that he takes leave of the disciples and ascends to heaven, and there the disciples remain gathered until he sends the Spirit upon them at Pentecost. Jerusalem is the birthplace of the Christian Church, and the movement in Acts is the opposite to that in Luke's Gospel: it is now an explosion outwards from Jerusalem to 'Judea and Samaria and to the end of the earth' (Acts 1.8).

On a road from Jerusalem to a nearby village, Emmaus, the post-Easter education of the disciples had begun: 'O foolish men, and slow of heart to believe all that the prophets have spoken! Was it not necessary that the Christ should suffer these things and enter into his glory?'(Luke 24.25-6). This episode is the essential sequel to the earlier challenge to the apostles, and to us: Who do you say that I am? What are your expectations? That challenge, and all Jesus's efforts to help them understand during his public life, were leading them to a new insight, but the insight was not *only* that they must let go of worldly hopes and selfish ambitions; that they must revise their idea of glory and look for it not in power and success but in humble, self-emptying,serviceable love. Certainly this was a necessary stage, but it was not the whole story. The apostles were not wrong in wanting God's Kingdom to be established on earth, only wrong about the time and manner of its coming. James and John were not in the long run disappointed. Jerusalem's hopes will be more than fulfilled. In the Emmaus story this lesson is driven home, for the first disciples and for us: your aims are not too high but too low; your plans are not excessively ambitious and grandiose but far too small and mean. They are a child's bauble of which you must let go; you cannot be like Peter Pan and remain a child for ever.

The Church has to learn Jesus's kind of glory, and from the first generation onwards it has meant unlearning other kinds. Once more Jerusalem's fortunes are symbolic. In the young community of Easter Christians at Jerusalem the Church celebrated a honeymoon, evoked by Luke in the early chapters of Acts and recalled with nostalgia by every generation since. In Paul's time the mother-church at Jerusalem was still the object of special veneration and generous charity, but the centre was shifting. Only by radiating outwards from Jerusalem, forgetting about privilege and prestige and putting itself at the service of the nations could the Church be faithful. In general it was. Cornelius was baptized, the Gentiles came pouring in without passing through the gateway of the Law, and Jewish privilege was soon only a memory. The Church found its true identity as the new Jerusalem only when it became universal in outlook; the little group who refused to do so, the 'Jerusalem church', became eventually a backwater, inward-looking and relatively unimportant. The real vision is evoked in the liturgy of the Epiphany:

> Arise, Jerusalem,
> rise clothed in light; your light has come
> and the glory of the Lord shines over you.
> For, though darkness covers the earth
> and dark night the nations,
> the Lord shall shine upon you
> and over you his glory appear;
> and the nations shall march towards your light
> and their kings to your sunrise. . . .
> Then you shall see, and shine with joy,
> then your heart shall thrill with pride. . . .
> Your gates shall open continually,
> they shall never be shut day or night.[10]

There is an inescapable connnection between this call to the Church to be the light of the nations and a sign of salvation for all, and its call to be the Servant Church. The apostles learnt the lesson, but the Church of every age has to relearn it. There are many ways in which this happens. It is very evident today that the Church has to be found on the side of the underprivileged and oppressed. Part of Israel's expectation was that the Messiah would right wrongs, defend the truth and establish a reign of justice:

> He shall not judge by what his eyes see,
> or decide by what his ears hear;
> but with righteousness he shall judge the poor,
> and decide with equity for the meek of the earth.
> (Isa. 11.3-4)

> He shall save the poor when they cry
> and the needy who are helpless.
> He will have pity on the weak
> and save the lives of the poor,
> From oppression he will rescue their lives,
> to him their blood is dear.
> (Ps. 72 (71).12–14, Grail)

All the efforts of Christ's followers to serve the cause of justice and peace, all the work of healing, liberation, education and care are part of the way in which God's reign is established. Its glory is to be seen within the brokenness of the human condition, where the compassion of those who are in any way on the side of Christ makes his love present, mediated through their own vulnerability and brokenness.

This is a world-transforming project, but it can begin only from the transformation of ourselves:

> Anoint the wounds
> of my spirit
> with the balm
> of forgiveness
> pour the oil
> of your calm
> on the waters
> of my heart

> take the squeal
> of frustration
> from the wheels
> of my passion
> that the power
> of your tenderness
> may smooth
> the way I love

that the tedium
of giving
in the risk
of surrender
and the reaching
out naked
to a world
that must wound

may be kindled
fresh daily
to a blaze
of compassion
that the grain
may fall gladly
to burst in the ground
– and the harvest abound.[11]

Painfully we have to unlearn our mistaken notions about glory, so that we can learn Christ's values and learn discipleship, consenting to serve and to be emptied and to let the light shine through us. For Christ's first nine months on earth Mary was his only visible medium; he shone only through her, as the sunlight shines with a special colour through the windows at Chartres. Today, believers are his transparencies. If the light is to come through we have to be servants of the covenant-love, wherever and in whatever way may be required, not for our own aggrandizement but in self-forgetting; and this is indeed glorious, although it does not feel like it. Jerusalem stands not only for the Church as a whole, but for every lover of God; 'and the city has no need of sun or moon to shine upon it, for the glory of God is its light, and its lamp is the Lamb' (Rev. 21.23). It is not your glory but his, and you have to consent to be transparent, to be the lantern not the light, like John the Baptist. Are you prepared to let this glory shine through you, through your unselfish loving, your smiling, your unselfseeking service and humility? Are you prepared to let the joy of the Lord radiate to others through you? In no other way will 'the glory of the Lord be revealed, and all mankind together see it'. It

123

will be visible only if we allow Christ to be born in our lives and shine through us.

Self-emptying love has to be learnt in prayer. Contemplation is the place for learning, because vulnerability to the love we meet there inexorably demands vulnerability and openness elsewhere. Regular confrontation with God in prayer purifies your love, your desire, your hope. The questions put by Jesus to the apostles are put to you too: What are your expectations? What kind of God are you meeting? You know what his glory is; do you want that? Are you prepared for such costly glory?

Mercifully, he is content with your dim desire to keep on following, as Jesus was with the loyalty of the apostles who stumbled after him on the road to Jerusalem, and he does not allow your hope to be disappointed, for it is of his own creating. He is leading you to glory. It works out in ordinariness, tedium, drabness, routine and the humdrum quality of most of our experience, and there is an overwhelming sense of how inglorious it all is. But the Spirit recycles this unpromising material, and the glory will be revealed in its time.

In the Christmas Gospels the word 'glory' shines through like a bright filigree. The shepherds are afraid when the glory of the Lord shines round them; the angels sing, 'Glory to God in the highest'; Simeon welcomes the child who is 'a light for revelation to the Gentiles and for glory to thy people Israel'; John tells us that 'the Word was flesh and we saw his glory'. But it is a dynamic glory that will work its way. There is no simple contrast between Old and New Testaments, as though the Old were all expectation and the New all fulfilment. For us too it is an unfinished tale. The glory of the Lord has not yet been fully revealed, nor has all mankind seen it, nor have the prophecies been fully realized, nor the reign of peace and righteousness established in power. But the glory of Christ's resurrection is let loose in the world and it is working. It is a process, furthered wherever people consent, even though in darkness and bewilderment, to his kind of glory.

8 Who is This?

One Word spoke the Father,
and this Word is his Son.
This Word speaks he ever in eternal silence,
and in silence must it be heard
by the soul. [1]

We live very close to a mysterious presence. God is 'nearer to me than myself', as St Augustine put it, but we do not see or understand him. He is utterly mysterious, and strangely gentle. When he makes himself known we are confounded, yet at the heart of our bewilderment there is a sense of recognizing something we have always known. There is nothing else quite like it in our whole experience.

There are traces of this in the Old Testament, where God walks with man in a strange homeliness. The same kind of experience is suggested by certain elements in the apostles' contacts with Jesus. Finally, our own experience of God bears the same hallmark. The purpose of this chapter is to evoke this elusive but unmistakable quality of his touch, a touch that stills us, the touch of the God who comes.

'Are you he who is to come, or must we look for another?' When the disciples of John the Baptist asked this of Jesus they were voicing the perennial question of a searching, waiting people. Israel had lived close to God for a very long time, listened to his word and truly known him, up to a point. But his self-giving revelation never exhausts his mystery. Faithful and constant, he is yet unpredictable, because his love is endlessly inventive and he is calling his beloved to a union beyond the horizons of human hope.

He led Israel from disillusionment to new vision, from disappointment to new-born hope, but always he was out ahead: Not this, not this. . . . They were the womb-community sheltering a mystery of love they had not seen, and from time to time they knew it:

> It will be said on that day, 'Lo, this is our God; we have waited for him, and he will save us. This is the Lord; we have waited for him, let us be glad and rejoice in his salvation.'
> (Isa. 25.9)

The 'Day of the Lord' would be terror, triumph, destruction, glory; the images multiplied, but it would above all be the manifestation of what was hidden, and it would be an encounter. Amos reminded an unheeding people of a series of calamities that should have brought them back to God in repentance, ending with a resounding command that meant more than he could have known: 'Prepare, O Israel, to meet your God' (Amos 4.12).

They believed that no one can see God and remain alive. Jacob wrestled with him in the dark, and the stronger one vanished before daybreak (cf. Gen. 32.24–31). Moses asked him straightforwardly, 'I pray thee, show me thy glory', but the Lord warned him, 'You cannot see my face; for man shall not see me and live' (Exod. 33.18, 20). Nevertheless, there is a strange gentleness amid the majesty, 'for I am God and not man, the Holy One in your midst, and I will not come to destroy' (Hos. 11.9). He transcends the signs of his own transcendence. Elijah met him outside a cave on a mountainside, and the Lord was not in the wind, nor in the earthquake, nor in the fire, but in a still, small voice (cf. 1 Kings 19.11–13). He is at home in his creation and his creatures can be strangely at home with him. There are many examples, but one of the best is Gideon's vision, in which 'the angel of the Lord' is the Lord himself; after calling Gideon to his task of leadership this 'angel of the Lord' touches the offerings Gideon has put before him, and they are immediately consumed by fire. Then

> Gideon perceived that he was the angel of the Lord; and . . . said, 'Alas, O Lord God! For now I have seen the angel of

the Lord face to face.' But the Lord said to him, 'Peace be to you; do not fear, you shall not die.' Then Gideon built an altar there to the Lord, and called it, The Lord is peace. (Judg. 6.22–4)

The apostles would have understood this. For about three years they lived close to a man they loved, sharing everything. He trusted them, taught them, needed them, challenged them, exploded with impatience at them and loved them; he commanded their total loyalty, yet they never completely understood him. They lived in close, daily, intimate companionship with a mysterious presence. He never held aloof from the physical, the ordinary, or the practicalities of life and work and human contacts, but there was something else about him, something that baffled them. There were moments when this other thing broke through; then they were awed and afraid, but he would swiftly reassure them with his ordinary kindness. One such occasion was when they were in a boat and a storm blew up, but he was so tired it did not even wake him. In their danger they cried to him, 'We're sinking! Don't you care?', an unceremonious form of address. 'And he awoke and rebuked the wind, and said to the sea, "Peace! Be still!" And the wind ceased, and there was a great calm' (Mark 4.39). To men familiar with the psalms the scene must have awakened echoes:

> [The Lord] spoke; he summoned the gale,
> tossing the waves of the sea
> up to heaven and back into the deep;
> their soul melted away in their distress.
> They staggered, reeled like drunken men,
> for all their skill was gone.
> Then they cried to the Lord in their need
> and he rescued them in their distress.
> He stilled the storm to a whisper:
> all the waves of the sea were hushed.
> They rejoiced because of the calm
> and he led them to the haven they desired.
> (Ps. 107 (106).25–30, Grail)

But that was Yahweh, the Lord who drove back the waters of chaos – and this was Jesus. They had a sense of the uncanny, or rather of the numinous: 'Who then is this, that even wind and sea obey him?' (Mark 4.41).

The Transfiguration was another such moment. He had gone off to pray, as he often did, but this time he took his three closest friends with him, perhaps because the pressures on him were very great, and even their uncomprehending presence was some comfort. Then something happened to him; perhaps it had happened before, but this time they were there to see it. In some way his longing love burst the barriers between mortality and immortality, and between the present moment and the past and future. Two men from distant ages were with him, talking with him about a death that supremely mattered to them, the death to which he was dedicating himself. The apostles saw the radiant Lord of life, as he would be when death was conquered, and they were terrified. It was like the shudder in the boat: 'Who *is* this?' But Jesus came and touched them, 'and said, "Stand up; do not be afraid." And when they raised their eyes they saw no one, but only Jesus' (Matt. 17.7–8, NEB). There is the same blend of transcendent mystery and easy kindness, and there is something unmistakable about it.

This impression is strongest in the resurrection stories, particularly as related by Luke and John. The Beyond is in the midst of them, but gentle, laughing, full of love, giving them his peace:

> Jesus himself stood among them, and said to them, 'Peace to you!' But they were startled and frightened, and supposed that they saw a spirit. And he said to them, 'Why are you troubled, and why do questionings arise in your hearts? See my hands and my feet, that it is I myself; handle me, and see, for a spirit has not flesh and bones as you see that I have.' And when he had said this, he showed them his hands and his feet. And while they still disbelieved for joy, and wondered, he said to them, 'Have you anything here to eat?'
> (Luke 24.36–43)

Sometimes he is simply there, as with the Emmaus travellers;

they hardly notice where he comes from and they do not seem to look at him carefully, though their hearts burn as he speaks to them. Only at the breaking of bread, the familiar gesture which Jesus has invested with unique significance, does the recognition dawn. It is similar for Mary Magdalene in the garden, and strongest of all, perhaps, in the lakeside scene. A huge catch, a man on the shore directing them – and John's intuition leaps up: 'It's the Lord!' But the rest of the episode is stranger. They go ashore, Jesus has got a fire going and has cooked breakfast for them. They eat together, as so often before. 'Now none of the disciples dared to ask him, "Who are you?" They knew it was the Lord' (John 21.12). The logic of that statement is very curious: because they knew who he was, they did not dare to ask. There is a unique clarity and light about these resurrection stories, and the oddity of this piece of logic is in keeping. There is mystery, awe, strangeness and an awareness of the Beyond; but the Beyond is quiet, friendly, gentle, considerate and perfectly at home. He is someone with whom you can have breakfast.

Only in the light of the resurrection did the apostles and the first Christian generation begin to find an answer to the question, 'Who is this?' The early sermons preserved in Acts, and some passages in Paul, reflect a stage of understanding at which the resurrection was seen as the moment when God himself proclaimed the identity of Jesus:

> This Jesus God raised up, and of that we all are witnesses. . . . Let all the house of Israel therefore know assuredly that God has made him both Lord and Christ, this Jesus whom you crucified.
> (Acts 2.32, 36)

> The gospel concerning [God's] Son, who was descended from David according to the flesh and designated Son of God in power according to the Spirit of holiness by his resurrection from the dead. . . .
> (Rom. 1.3–4)

Further Christian reflection, already well advanced before the Gospels were written, worked retroactively, reading

129

back into the time of Jesus's ministry some recognition by the apostles that he was Son of God. Pushing back a little further, Mark presented Jesus's baptism as a decisive moment when his divine sonship was attested by the Father's voice and the descent of the Spirit. Mark is not suggesting that Jesus *became* Son of God at his baptism; this is a moment of attestation of what he truly is. But Mark does not show it as generally recognized by the bystanders. Rather he presents a two-stage Christology by which what Jesus is, even during his public life, is recognized only at his crucifixion.[2]

By the time Matthew and Luke wrote, evaluation of who Jesus is had been pushed back further still: he was Son of God from the first moment of his (human) life. The Infancy Gospels of Matthew and Luke tell us, each in its own way, the truth of his identity. Jesus is Son of David and so the awaited Davidic Messiah, but he is also Son of God.[3]

This movement backwards in christological thinking bifurcated, however. John has no Infancy Gospel, but his answer to the question, 'Who is Jesus?' is a clear assertion of divine pre-existence. Jesus is the eternal Word, the only-begotten Son of God from all eternity, who takes flesh and begins to exist as a man on a day in time.[4] The Johannine Christ himself implicitly answers the all-important question, even during his mortal life, with language which to Jewish ears had unmistakable divine overtones: 'Before Abraham was, I am.'[5]

Yet for John too the paschal event is crucial to the revelation of who Jesus is, since it is the Spirit sent by the glorified Christ who 'receives from what is his and shows it to us' (cf. John 16.14). On that day, Jesus promises, 'You will know that I am in my Father, and you in me, and I in you' (John 14.20). The day of which he speaks is the day of Easter, the day of God's self-giving to us through the Spirit of the Easter Christ. It is the 'Day of the Lord' to which the prophets looked; it stretches from Easter to Christ's final coming, and we walk in it in newness of life.

God is like Jesus. His touch in our lives has the same self-authenticating quality of rightness. He is not pretentious, and our complications fall away before his simplicity. His gentleness and mercy may bowl us over, but we can be ourselves with him, more than anywhere else, 'For in us', said Julian of Norwich, 'is his homeliest home and his endless dwelling.'[6]

Yet God is always surprising. The God who is, who was and who is to come is always out ahead of us. Christ was unexpected, for the most part, at his first coming, despite the long preparation. He will presumably be unexpected at his final coming. In between these events are his many comings in grace, and they too are surprising. Like the Jews, we tend to look for the wrong things, expecting him to fit our categories, our vision and our needs. It was the Gentiles at Athens who put up an altar 'To an Unknown God' (cf. Acts 17.23); the Jews would not have thought of doing so. That was part of the Advent of the Gentiles, but there is a real sense in which it applied to the Jews as well. Our lives too are an Advent, and we look for the known yet still unknown God, whose self-giving does not diminish his mystery.

We know God in darkness; we meet him in a cloud of unknowing; we know more truly what he is not than what he is; we know him by love. These are the constant teachings of a powerful stream of Christian contemplative tradition. Its fountainhead is St Gregory of Nyssa in the fourth century, who wrote of Moses's encounter with God in the cloud at Sinai, seeing in it the Christian's growth towards contemplative union. The tradition was furthered by the anonymous Neo-Platonist Christian writer of the fifth century known as Pseudo-Dionysius. He gave a powerful impetus to 'apophatic theology'; that is, the theology of denial, for whatever affirmation we make about God, he says, must be immediately qualified with 'But he is *not* like that'. In the fourteenth century the same current flowed in Western Europe, in the great Rhineland mystics and especially in the sane, robust, anonymous author of *The Cloud of Unknowing*. In sixteenth-century Spain St John of the Cross, heir to all these, brought the tradition to a fine flowering.

The indwelling Trinity transforms the human spirit at its highest, or deepest, reality. God perfects the human intellect

131

by the gift of faith, a power beyond its natural powers which enables it to reach out to God and touch him, beyond the natural scope of its knowing yet without violence to its integrity. The will of man, oriented by its nature to what is good and capable of desiring God, is perfected by the gift of charity, a share in God's own love and a desire for self-surrendering union with God who is love. In contemplative prayer these God-given faculties are like antennae, truly putting us in touch with God. The ordinary activity of the intellect can 'jam' the prayer if not controlled, so the mystics speak of darkness and silence, and of the renunciation of our clear, formulated ideas about God in the time of prayer. Contemplative union is his gracious gift, and on our side we seek him by 'a blind stirring of love unto God for himself',[7] by a 'naked intent unto God' which presses upon the dark cloud of unknowing that separates us from him, for 'I would leave all that thing that I can think, and choose to my love that thing I cannot think. For why; he may well be loved, but not thought. By love may he be gotten and holden, but by thought never.'[8]

It must be remembered that all the writers mentioned were firmly within the Catholic tradition, themselves trained theologians who took for granted the doctrine, sacraments, life and discipline of the Church and presumed the same grounding in their disciples. There is no anti-intellectualism here. Their minds were fed, inspired and guided by the Scriptures, the liturgy and the wealth of symbolism which were the common heritage of Christian believers. Nevertheless, there is a certain difference of emphasis between these 'theologians of darkness' and others who are often considered 'theologians of light', like John, Paul, Augustine, Bernard and many in the monastic tradition. Apophatic theology and spirituality are a necessary reminder of the mystery and hiddenness of God, and of the inadequacy of any representation of him. This tradition of prayer is one of the ways by which we are saved from our sophisticated idolatries.

I said to my soul, be still, and let the dark come upon you
Which shall be the darkness of God. . . .

I said to my soul, be still, and wait without hope
For hope would be hope for the wrong thing; wait without
   love
For love would be love of the wrong thing; there is yet faith
But the faith and the love and the hope are all in the waiting.
Wait without thought, for you are not yet ready for thought:
So the darkness shall be the light, and the stillness the
   dancing.[9]

Anyone who regularly prays, and is willing to take the
consequences of doing so, is likely to become aware of the
invitation, 'Be still and know that I am God' (Ps. 46 (45).11,
Grail). Silence is not simply negation but presence to the
Beloved, receptivity, awareness and availability. Silence is
the attitude by which we honour the reality of God. St
Ephrem catches the spirit of it:

A thousand thousands stand,
thousands and ten thousands are not able to search into
   the One,
for all of them stand in silence to minister.
No one can comprehend him save the Son who is from
   him,
within his silence alone can there be inquiry into his
   nature.
If the angels had come to search
they would have met the Silence and been restrained. . . .
Shall one feel thee with his hands,
when there is not even a mind keen enough to feel
   after thee . . .?
Shall one listen to thee with the ears,
when thou art more fearful than thunder?
Thou art a stillness that cannot be heard,
a silence that cannot be listened to.
Shall a man see thee with his eyes,
when thou art the bright Morning Light?
From all is the sight of thee concealed. . . .
Let us ask the angels who stand near thy gate.
Though the angels stand before thee with praises,
yet they know not where to look for thee.

133

> They sought thee above in the height, they saw thee in the
> depth;
> they searched for thee in heaven, they saw thee in the deep;
> they looked for thee with the Adorable One, they found
> thee amid creatures;
> they came down to thee and gave thee praise. . . .
> Wondrous art thou, wherever we seek thee.
> Thou art near and far off, who shall approach thee?
> Faith alone finds thee, and love with prayer.[10]

If you are to be able to respond to the invitation in prayer, 'Be still', you need a measure of silence in your life. In today's world silence is in short supply; this is a serious problem for our society, and anything we can do to help people recover a sense of silence as a necessary and positive element in human life is a contribution to the general sanity. Many people can, however, contrive some islands of silence in their lives, perhaps in holiday time. Without romantically ignoring our dependence on our environment it is also true to say that silence is partly an interior quality; you can learn to live from your own deep centre, rather than in the ego with its clamorous demands. You can make positive use of any period of silence that does occur, rather than looking on it as an empty stretch of time to be endured or filled up somehow. Silence like this is not a threat to us but an invitation to depth, to listening, to a loving communion in joy. It lays us open to the strong creativity of the Spirit, and he is the Spirit both of contemplation and of outgoing love. Contemplation, trust and reaching out to people go together. Mary's silent surrender to God at the Annunciation sent her swiftly out in the generous and practical love of the Visitation. Christ is in you, yours to give, a quiet light.

It may help us, when we are painfully conscious of turmoil, to remember that Christ's gifts are more than a spiritualized version of secular commodities. As the love he gives us is a love that has made itself vulnerable to all that hatred can do and has conquered hatred, as the life he gives is a life that has been through death and proved the stronger, so the peace he gives is something more than an absence of stress: 'Peace I leave with you; my peace I give to you; not as the world gives do I give to you' (John 14.27). The gift may sometimes be offered and received within the turmoil, in the eye of the storm.

Christian contemplation can never leave Jesus behind. However simplified and imageless prayer may become, however close the mystical union with God who is beyond all comprehension, it is Christ's incarnation and redemption that make them possible. St Teresa of Avila never gave up meditating on the Lord's passion to the end of her life. St John of the Cross, describing the mystical marriage at the summit of contemplative union, asserts that in this state the soul understands the mysteries of faith in a new way, for the Lord 'communicates to it the sweet mysteries of his incarnation and the ways and manners of human redemption'.[11] Jesus is the revealer of the Father and the giver of the Spirit of prayer: 'No one comes to the Father but by me. If you had known me, you would have known my Father also. . . . He who has seen me has seen the Father. . . . Do you not believe that I am in the Father and the Father in me?' (John 14.6, 7, 9, 10). The Last Discourse reported by John is Jesus's 'intolerable wrestle with words and meanings', and here if anywhere language cracks under the strain. But he does truly reveal the Father, and we do really know amid all the bafflement and unknowing.

If you are called to contemplative prayer, which is not some esoteric adventure for the very few but by God's grace a normal flowering of baptismal life, you have to live in day-to-day fidelity to mysteries you do not fully understand, like Mary. This is what Advent is about, but it is also a general law of our lives, which are an Advent. You have to wait in hope, waiting for the mystery to unfold, going on doing ordinary things but all the time listening, learning, pondering, growing and energetically serving. You have to be silent before the mystery. In the Book of Job the 'comforters' are the ones who cannot be silent before it but must rush in with their explanations. You know your kinship with the mystery. By your closeness to Christ his mind is being formed in you, and he is leading you into his own experience, his own

135

joy and longing, and his own knowledge of the Father. Whatever the renunciations, the inner poverty and the successive little deaths and lettings-go, this life of contemplation is a life of joy, because lived in Jesus it is a journey into God, an unfinished tale.

As you ponder the word in your heart, like Mary pondering all her life mysteries she served and adored but did not fully understand, you are the Church. Like Israel, the Church is the womb-community sheltering mysteries not yet seen. The Church has received the word, but must give it life within its own life, and let the word speak and speak again through every age and culture in its inexhaustible fullness. The Spirit leads the Church into the contemplation of what has been given in Christ. The Second Vatican Council's *Constitution on Divine Revelation* spoke of this:

> There is a growth in insight into the realities and words that are being passed on. This comes about in various ways. It comes through the contemplation and study of believers who ponder these things in their hearts. It comes from the intimate sense of spiritual realities which they experience. And it comes from the preaching of those who have received, along with their right of succession to the episcopate, the sure charism of truth. Thus, as the centuries go by, the Church is always advancing towards the plenitude of divine truth, until eventually the words of God are fulfilled in her.[12]

It will take the whole time of history to hear that word. The Church is the place for asking questions about Christ. We are in the same boat as the apostles. Who *is* this? The Church must always be asking this question, asking it through every available channel of understanding, asking it anew through the minds of every age, asking it with the utmost breadth, depth, clarity and seriousness. Contemplation is one of the ways through which faith seeks understanding. Like Jacob, contemplatives wrestle with God in the dark: 'Tell me your name. Who are you?' (cf. Gen. 32.29). And then, in daylight, there is the further wrestle with words and meanings, to translate into forms that can be communicated what has been an immediate intuition of love. Contemplative theology is part of the Spirit's gift of wisdom; it is a savouring of divine realities, an understanding by kinship or 'connaturality'. The Church needs contemplatives, and so does the world.

Contemplative prayer is the work of the Spirit at the heart of the Church, which is to say at the heart of human persons alive in Christ. It is a means whereby he draws us into the mystery of salvation which is accomplished in Christ's Easter. We are called to live the redemptive mysteries of which we read in the Scriptures, which the Church professes in the Creed and celebrates in the liturgy; or rather, we are called to allow Christ to live them in us and celebrate his passover in our lives. For the Christian Fathers contemplation was an ecclesial reality, a necessary element in the story of salvation which is unfolding and moving towards its fulfilment in the life of the Church. The whole Church, new-born in Christ by baptism, is engaged in a continuous process of conversion, which is the condition for meeting God. The life of the Church is ruled and inspired by the scriptural word of God, and so the mysticism of the Fathers is rooted in the Bible and the sacraments. Personal, individual experience of God granted to members of the Church is the expected and necessary prolongation or unfolding of the word and the history which are the Church's life.

This knowing, this listening, goes on at the centre and heart of our most personal life and prayer, it can go on in every experience of our lives, however apparently unpromising, and it goes on in the fellowship of believers, as the Letter to the Ephesians makes plain:

> According to the riches of his glory [may the Father] grant you to be strengthened with his might through the Spirit in the inner man . . . that Christ may dwell in your hearts through faith; that you, being rooted and grounded in love, may have power to comprehend *with all the saints* what is the breadth and length and height and depth, and *to know the love of Christ which surpasses knowledge*, that you may be filled with all the fulness of God.
> (Eph. 3.16–19)

The Church too goes on doing things faithfully, guarding truth and fostering holiness and caring for sinners, sometimes without perfectly knowing why; the meaning of some part of the tradition may be discovered or rediscovered after centuries. This is even true of the fulfilment of the command, 'Do this in memory of me'. What 'this' is has not yet been fully understood. We can say much, and then fall silent. The Church is showing forth the death of the Lord until he comes.

This is partly why we keep Advent. There is a mysterious, poetic, oblique quality about it, because Advent makes use of many symbols and is itself a great symbol. It is of the nature of a symbol to evoke more than it directly reveals, and to invite participation. Through the focus of one reality other realities are seen. In Advent the preparation for the feast of Christ's coming as man broadens into a wondering contemplation of the mystery of the God who comes. Who *is* he? We live always with a mysterious presence, and in Advent we celebrate it. The question in the boat is asked, meditatively. A few liturgical texts chosen almost at random may serve to evoke this:

> Behold, the Lord shall come, and all his holy ones with him: then the eyes of the blind shall be opened, and the ears of the deaf unstopped. Then shall the lame man leap like a hart and the tongue of the dumb sing for joy. . . . Behold, the Lord God comes with might, and his arm rules for him. . . . Then shall the lame man leap like a hart, and the tongue of the dumb sing for joy.

> He has entered before us and on our behalf, the Lamb, holy and undefiled. He has become a high priest of the order of Melchizedek, and for ever. . . . This is the King of righteousness, he has neither beginning of days nor end of life. . . . He has become a high priest of the order of Melchizedek, and for ever.

> When the Lord has given you the bread of suffering and the water of distress, he who is your teacher will hide no longer, and you will see your teacher with your own

eyes. Whether you turn to right or to left, your ears will hear these words behind you, 'This is the way, follow it'.

O that thou wouldst rend the heavens and come down. . . .!

He shall come into Bethlehem, walking upon the waters of the redemption of Judah. Then shall every one be saved, for behold, he comes.

Arise, Jerusalem, stand on the heights, and see the joy that is coming to you from God.

Advent is primarily about the coming of God, and only in a secondary way about our asking, seeking, waiting and longing. There is hope, because we are unconditionally loved, whatever may be our failures, our tepidity or our secret despair. The word 'Come' is a bearer of mystery. It resounds through Scripture, through the prayer of the Church and – not always articulate but real – through the hidden liturgy of the world's history. God says 'Come', to man; man says 'Come', to God. In various specific contexts, we say it to Jesus and to the Spirit. It is the word of lovers. In the Song of Songs the bridegroom says to the bride:

> Rise up, my darling;
> my fairest, come away. . . .
> Let me see your face, let me hear your voice;
> for your voice is pleasant, your face is lovely.
> (2.13, 14, NEB)

The Bride-Church, particularly in the liturgy of Advent, prays, 'Come, show us thy face', recalling Moses's plea to God, 'Show me thy glory'. Faces are relational. The word 'Come' is also relational throughout the love poetry of the world and throughout its prayer; it is the singing together of the two loves.

'Come' is God's creative word to us. He calls us into being at our first creation, into the light of life. All our lives we are creatures of becoming, always incomplete, always growing (or regressing), always pilgrims and discoverers. We are

finding our way to our destiny by our choices, our orienta-
tions, and our decisions about where to set our love. This is
the law of our creation, and still more the law of our new
creation, whereby God calls us out of darkness into his
marvellous light. Revelation and salvation are a love affair in
which God says, 'Come', to humankind, calling us to come
and see him as he is, and share his life.

The Old Testament people heard that word at a few very
crucial moments: at the summons to come out of Egypt and
follow the Lord of the wilderness, and again at the end of the
exile in Second Isaiah's call, 'Come out of Babylon!' (Isa.
48.20). They heard it in a particular way through the same
prophet's assertion of the sheer gratuitousness of salvation:

> Every one who thirsts, come to the waters:
> and he who has no money, come, buy and eat!
> Come, buy wine and milk without money and without
> price.
> (Isa. 55.1)

Israel's response, when it was most typically and truly
itself, was an answering 'Come' to God. The God who made
himself known to them as Yahweh is a God who says 'I am
here', or 'I will be there'; he is the God who comes. The
prophets spoke of his reign or kingdom which was coming,
and it was the Spirit who spoke through the prophets. The
whole immense aspiration of mankind towards the God who
comes, the aspiration focused in Israel, was fostered by the
Spirit.

Jesus says significant things in John's Gospel about why
he has come. To Pilate he testifies: 'For this I was born, and
for this I have come into the world, to bear witness to the
truth' (John 18.37). As the Good Shepherd he claims, 'I came
that they may have life, and have it abundantly' (John 10.10).
The official at Capernaum whose son is ill says to Jesus, with
overtones of ampler meaning as so often in this Gospel, 'Sir,
come down before my child dies' (John 4.49), to be met with
Jesus's immediate response, 'Your son will live'.

Even more significant is Jesus's own use of the word
'Come' when as man he offers God's invitation to men.

'Come, follow me', is his call to those he has chosen to be apostles, and to any who are willing to take up their cross and be his disciples. The call is also a promise, for his followers are invited to 'Come and see'; their following will take them in the end to the vision of God. The will to follow is, however, no merely human decision, but sheer grace; only a person drawn by the Father can 'come', because to come to Jesus is to believe in him and faith is a gift: 'No one can come to me unless the Father who sent me draws him' (John 6.44). The initial invitation and response are followed by many another call, 'Come', as we are asked to let go of our securities and stake our all on the power and fidelity of God made present in Jesus. A vivid image of this is Jesus's summons to Peter to come to him across the water. One of the most powerful of Jesus's invitations is that described by John at the raising of Lazarus, a 'sign' that points towards Jesus's own resurrection and the truth of his claim that he himself is the resurrection and the life. Into the grave of a man dead four days he shouts, 'Lazarus, come out!' (John 11.43). All the power and mystery of God's call to sinful, mortal man are in that cry.

With the conviction of the first Christians that in Jesus the promises were fulfilled and the God of Israel truly present, the dynamism of the Old Testament might have been expected to slow down. It did not. In the New Testament hope is stronger than ever. Christ has come as Saviour, but he will come again in glory, and the Kingdom of God which is already hidden among us will be manifested. The longing for this final triumph of God's love in human beings and in the cosmos was central to Jesus's own prayer and to the prayer he taught his disciples: 'Thy kingdom come'. The coming of the Kingdom 'does not admit of observation' (Luke 17.20, JB), for it is within us and among us; nevertheless, there will be a sudden, unexpected coming, for which we are bidden to watch. Constantly through the preaching of Jesus the note of urgency is sounded, the warning to be alert. We are in the situation of servants whose master is abroad but will return unexpectedly, or of bridesmaids awaiting the bridegroom who has been delayed and arrives at midnight.

The Lord will come like a thief in the night, and it is advisable to stay awake. This night watch is an essential element in Christian life; the Church keeps vigil for him.

His coming is now. In the Last Discourse he promises an interior coming into the inmost hearts of his friends which will be the consequence of his resurrection and his gift of the Spirit: 'I will not leave you desolate; I will come to you' (John 14.18). This coming will be an indwelling of Father and Son in those who love him: 'If a man loves me, he will keep my word, and my Father will love him, and we will come to him and make our home with him' (John 14.23). Similar to this is the tender promise of the risen Christ in the Book of Revelation: 'Behold, I stand at the door and knock; if anyone hears my voice and opens the door, I will come in to him and eat with him, and he with me' (Rev. 3.20). The meeting of lovers is real already, but they look for a consummation beyond this life, and it too is promised: 'When I go and prepare a place for you, I will come again and take you to myself, that where I am you may be also' (John 14.3). For each of us there will be the Lover's call, 'Come', at our death, and for his midnight coming all our life is a preparation. But the promise that he will come again sustains the hope of the whole Church. Beyond the struggle and the failure, beyond the confusion and the glories of human history and the Church's immersion in it, there stands the Lord's promise: he will come again to claim his victory in its fullness and reveal God's reign. The New Testament closes with the Church's prayer, 'Come, Lord Jesus! *Marana tha*' (Rev. 22.20).

Advent is the symbolic, sacramental expression of this reality of the Church's being, the waiting, hoping, expectant Church, the Church of vigil and joy who knows that 'the best is yet to be'. The poetical texts that articulate Advent prayer are sometimes directly quoted from Scripture, but with their bearing changed; examples of this have been given already in this chapter, and there is a rightness in the Church's massive adoption and reinterpretation of so much of the Old Testament at this time. Sometimes they are interweavings of different texts, or adaptations that catch the mood: 'Come,

Lord, do not delay, visit your people in peace'; or, 'Come, Lord, visit us in peace, that we may rejoice in your presence with hearts made whole'.

In all this movement of the lovers towards each other, the Spirit is the active, creative source. Through the Spirit the risen Christ comes to us in this in-between time that separates the resurrection from the parousia. He is the mode of Jesus's presence now, and in this sense the Church prays, 'Come, Holy Spirit'. But the marvellous truth is that the Spirit is on both ends of this 'Come' dialogue; he has been aptly called 'the Go-Between God'. As God he speaks the inviting 'Come' to human beings: 'Let him who is thirsty come, let him who desires take the water of life without price' (Rev. 22.17). The living water is the symbol of the Spirit himself, and St Ignatius of Antioch in the second century, on his way to martyrdom, testified to the Spirit's invitation: 'There is a living water speaking within me, saying, "Come to the Father".'[13]

Yet the Spirit is also the creative source of man's responsive 'Come' to God. He inspires and sustains the Church's prayer and hope: 'The Spirit and the Bride say, "Come." And let him who hears say, "Come"' (Rev. 22.17). It is parallel to his work in the prophets during the Old Testament, but stronger now. He longs in the hearts of God's people, and in our prayer, for the meeting of the lovers:

> For we do not know how to pray as we ought, but the Spirit himself intercedes for us with sighs too deep for words. And he who searches the hearts of men knows what is the mind of the Spirit, because the Spirit intercedes for the saints according to the will of God.
> (Rom. 8.26–7)

The Spirit, who is God, is praying. He is praying 'according to the will of God'. He is praying in the heart of the Church, 'Come, Lord Jesus'; that is, he who is God, who is the bond of union between Father and Son, is 'praying' for the consummation, for the final takeover that will be the fulfilment of all humankind's longings. And our prayer is a part of this activity. It is small wonder if we feel out of our depth.

143

Who is Jesus? Who is God? The Church goes on asking the question. It will be finally answered when he comes to tell us himself.

9 The Final Coming

Where is the flower of my desire,

Absolve me, God, that in the land
Which I can nor regard nor know
Nor think about nor understand,
The flower of my desire shall blow.[1]

The Christian Fathers delighted to speak of three comings of Christ. At his first coming he was wrapped in swaddling clothes and laid in a manger, at his last he will be clothed in light as in a garment; at his first coming he endured the cross, despising the shame, at his last he will be exalted in majesty. In between these two there is a secret coming in the lives of all who will receive him. His first advent was in the flesh and in weakness; his secret advent now is in spirit and in power; his final advent will be in the open glory of God.

The three comings are linked. In the twelfth century the Cistercian abbot Guerric of Igny expressed the connections like this in an Advent sermon:

> As our bodies will rise up rejoicing at his final coming, so our hearts must run joyfully to greet his first. . . . Between these two comings of his, the Lord often visits each one of us in accordance with our merits and desires, forming us to the likeness of his first coming in the flesh, and preparing us for his return at the end of time. He comes to us now to make sure that his first coming shall not have been wasted, and that his last coming may not have to be in anger. His purpose now is to convert our pride into the humility he showed when he first came, so that hereafter he may refashion our lowly bodies into the likeness of that glorious body which he will manifest when he comes again. . . . Grace accompanied his first coming, glory will surround his

last; this intermediate coming has in it something of both, since by it we experience in the consolations of his grace a foretaste of his glory.[2]

Advent is the celebration of all three comings, but so far most of our attention has been given to the first two: God's self-gift to the world through Israel at the incarnation, and his self-gift to each believer personally. Now comes the difficult task of saying something about the final coming. As an event it is, unlike the other two, still outside our experience, but the New Testament hope that Christ will come again is in some way earthed in our own expectations, fears and desires.

If modern men and women are to be more than simply agnostic about the long-term prospects for our race, their most fundamental hope must be that it will not end in meaningless destruction. If we are going to blow ourselves out of existence as though we had never been, or make our planet uninhabitable without finding alternative accommodation, there is little point in hoping for anything else. To believe that the human race will eventually reach the end of its earthly pilgrimage is one thing; to equate the end with total, blind destruction is another. It is sad that the latter prospect is what many moderns term 'apocalyptic', if they use the word at all.

The hope that we are travelling towards a destiny, rather than a mere collapse, is linked with the faith that our origins were already purposeful. If we think that our existence is a mere fluke, the result of some wildly improbable mix in some primal soup that threw up the conditions required to sustain life, then our whole human story is a chance bubble; it has no purpose and can be pricked as meaninglessly as it was formed. But if there is a Creator who stands outside the whole cosmic evolutionary process, and yet works his will within it by a wisdom and love that are present in its every tiniest movement, then human life has a purpose. It begins from God and is on its way to a goal which, however unimaginable, will give meaning to the whole adventure.

We cannot comfort ourselves with wishful thinking. We

instinctively admire the courage of those who squarely face the possibility that human life is simply absurd, that there is no future at all, and that the only honourable option is to live with dignity and kindness as we wait for our meaningless extinction. Courageous as it is, however, this view is not convincing, for it leaves too much unexplained. Deeply rooted in our experience is an obstinate certainty that our best intuitions will prove to have been the truest, and no mockery. We also want justice, however we may fear it or fall short in practising it ourselves. Our hearts demand that the very rough and uneven scheme of distribution in this life shall be redeemed within a larger justice.

A very radical conviction is in us that good, not evil, will triumph in the end. The classic fairytales conclude with the assurance that the wicked are defeated and everyone else lives happily ever after. They appeal because they strike a chord in us. It is true that sophisticated modern novels and short stories often eschew the neat, satisfactory ending, preferring to leave us in the air with a question in our minds. But this is not really a denial of the intuition that good will conquer evil in the long run; it is only a distrust of the too-hasty, facile solution which in order neatly to tie up the ends bypasses too many of the facts of life. We feel that the final settlement must be larger than that. Even within the fairytale the traditional happy ending is reached only through suffering, danger, courage and endurance. No *deus ex machina* solution will satisfy our deepest desires; we could not rest content with an end which was mere comforting, the awakening from a bad dream to find that all the evil has been unreal after all. We know that if our instinct for truth is to be trusted, the whole sin of the world in which we are all accomplices must be taken with absolute, ultimate seriousness, and shown up for what it is in the light of God's holiness. Only so will our own responsibility and freedom be respected.

It is not difficult for us today to believe in the reality of evil and its power to wreak havoc. We remain responsible for the future of our race and our planet. Statements of Christian faith that fall into naive optimism, or fail to take that responsibility seriously, or seek to domesticate evil, are not fully credible; nor are they the best way to honour the God who has given us reason to think that he himself takes evil very seriously indeed. None the less, the witness of inspired hope remains.

The New Testament has a good deal to say about the final coming of the Lord which will signal the end. The data are of two kinds. On the one hand there are apocalyptic passages in the Synoptics, in St Paul and in other Epistles, to which certain parables are akin; and, on the other, there is eschatological teaching with a different emphasis to be found in St John. Moreover, the One who is coming, on whose will and character our destiny depends, is no stranger. Although his final coming will be the termination of history, and therefore not commensurate with events inside history, there are certain constant factors in his dealings with us. This chapter will try to pick up the various hints.

The Synoptic Gospels and some of the Epistles use elaborate and fairly stereotyped imagery in an attempt to convey the unstatable and unimaginable reality of the coming of God in judgement at the end-time. The scenario includes angels, trumpets, the resurrection of the dead, stars falling from heaven, the sun and moon going out, wars, famines, plagues, earthquakes, lightning and the glorious coming of the Son of Man upon the clouds to judge mankind. This imagery was derived from the seventh chapter of the Book of Daniel and became common in the apocalyptic writings of late Judaism. There is a parallel between it and the imagery used by earlier writers to convey their message about the beginnings. There we had a seven-day creation, a creative word of God calling things into being and establishing a cosmic order, then a garden and a fellowship between God and man. Here we have the breakdown of the cosmic order amid terrors and portents of judgement. In both cases the medium is a culturally conditioned set of images, and we have to try to hear the message with our differently conditioned minds. It may be objected that the question, 'What is it saying?' is illegitimate, since the medium is intrinsic to the message, but we have to listen to the word with the minds we have and, as we shall see, there is reinterpretation of this apocalyptic eschatology even within the New Testament.

The central affirmation of the New Testament apocalyptic passages is that Christ will come to judge a sinful world. This divine judgement will involve the collapse of the created order into chaos, but it will be above all a vindication of the holiness and glory of God. From it will issue a new creation in which the promises of salvation will be realized. In some of these passages there is a mingling of perspectives; parts of Jesus's discourse concern the destruction of Jerusalem in AD 70, while other parts refer to the end of time. One 'judgement' is seen through the focus of another. The destruction of Jerusalem prefigures the final judgement, because it is the end of an era; it is literally 'epoch-making'. It brings the period of the old covenant to an end, and so the judgement of Israel typifies the judgement of mankind that will end all history.

There are analogies between different 'judgements' of God in the story of salvation; between, for instance, the flood, the Babylonian invasion in the sixth century BC, and the destruction of Jerusalem by the Romans. Each time there is a picture of sin, of a whole corrupt order of things in which God's will is ignored and rejected. Catastrophe falls upon the guilty society, fearful chastisement is meted out and the old order crumbles into chaos. But each time there is forgiveness and the gift of a new beginning, and each time the seed of the new creation has been sown within the old. To make the point clear we need to look at these themes in the three instances just mentioned.

The flood is presented by Genesis as a punishment sent by God:

> The Lord saw that the wickedness of man was great in the earth, and that every imagination of the thoughts of his heart was only evil continually. And the Lord was sorry that he had made man on earth, and it grieved him to his heart. So the Lord said, 'I will blot out man whom I have created

> from the face of the ground, man and beast and creeping
> things and birds of the air, for I am sorry that I have made
> them'.
> (Gen. 6.5–7)

It is man who has corrupted and destroyed creation first; the
outward cataclysm is only a ratification of what he has done:
'Now the earth was corrupt in God's sight, and the earth was
filled with violence' (Gen. 6.11). So the ever-threatening but
hitherto restrained waters are let loose and the ordered
cosmos engulfed; chaos has returned. But before this
happens, Noah is there, and 'Noah was righteous man,
blameless in his generation; Noah walked with God' (Gen.
6.9). He obeys God and he is saved, and from him springs
the new race, the remnant with whom God makes a new
beginning. Noah and his family are blessed and ordered to
be fruitful and multiply, as Adam and Eve were at the
beginning. With them God makes a covenant (cf. Gen.
9.8–17). The story of salvation enters a new phase.

During the period of the Israelite monarchy, from the
eleventh to the sixth century BC, the purpose of kingship and
of the state organization which grew up round it was to
promote obedience to the will of God. Yahweh was the true
king of Israel, the earthly monarch only his vicegerent.
Under David and one or two later kings it realized its
purpose, but more often it led the people into sin, and thus
made itself meaningless and ultimately dispensable. Before
the Babylonian invasion Judah and Jerusalem, and even
the temple itself, were thoroughly corrupt. Siege, capture,
devastation and exile followed; Babylon was God's scourge.
But already within the old order the 'anawim were there, poor
and praying, hopeful and humble, the spiritual kernel of the
nation, and to them the future belonged. The seed of the new
had been quietly planted within the old before its collapse.

The Jewish religious establishment in the time of Jesus
could not, for a variety of reasons, open itself to the gift of
God that his coming represented. It perceived his teaching
and his implicit claims as subversive, and rejected, in the
name of the whole people, this supreme and crucial call to

obedience. In so doing it condemned itself, and seemingly forfeited its privileged role in the story of salvation.[4] The abrogation of God's covenant with Israel-according-to-the-flesh was outwardly symbolized by the sacking of the holy city and the temple by the army of Titus, but the seed of the new people had been sown already by the events of Jesus's passover some forty years earlier. The Church, the new Israel, had been born in Jerusalem, but had by this time found new centres at Antioch and throughout the Mediterranean world.

If, then, these constant characteristics are to be found in the various judgements of God within history, it is legitimate to see them as models for the final judgement that will end history. At the same time the recurrent picture is familiar, for it corresponds to our own experience. There is a sinful society and way of life, in which God's will is flouted and unfaith dominates. Although men and women are to some extent conscious of the evil (for were they not, it would be no sin) the full destructiveness and perversion of evil are not manifest. Because few people are walking with God in the light of his holiness, much of the sin is masked. There is opacity, ambiguity, falsehood, twisted thinking and the deadening of consciences. Sin is not fully revealed for what it is.

Then comes a cataclysm in the shape of flood or war or invasion, producing visible, tangible, horrible chaos. It does not really cause the chaos, but reveals what has been there all along in a latent form. Sin is the true cause of the chaos; the external disaster shows up the essentially negative and destructive character of disobedience to God and refusal of his love. The prospect of our repeating this pattern is almost too horrible to contemplate, yet we know it is a possibility. Modern technology has the power to unleash destruction greater than the world has ever seen, but it is not material things as such which are evil. Destruction wrought by man lays bare what is in our society and in our hearts. It is a sign of sin, because sin is ultimately self-destructive, individually or racially.

In this perspective we can perhaps come a little nearer to understanding the 'anger' of God which is an element in popular thinking about the final judgement. The *Dies Irae* and various medieval art-forms expressed it in their own idiom; they were affirming something real, but the idiom may not altogether help us. It is clear that God is not some irate, capricious despot hurling his thunderbolts. He is the God who has made us for himself and given us freedom so that we can love and respond, the God who respects our freedom to such a point that he will not in the end override it. The fearful possibility therefore exists of ultimate self-frustration on our part: the abiding choice of hatred, the determined closing-in on self, the definitive refusal of love by a creature whose whole structure and meaning is to be an open relationship since in its finite measure it is modelled on the Persons of the Trinity. This would be self-chosen hell. Hell cannot be anything but self-chosen.

Everything suggested so far belongs to a picture of creation dislocated by sin; that is, to a picture of sinful man, in a world perverted by his sin, *vis-à-vis* the holy God. This, however, is by no means the whole story. The primary affirmation of New Testament apocalyptic is not that sin works itself out but that God intervenes. Because of some unprecedented act of God a wholly new situation comes into being, which is not simply the development of what went before.

By 'sending his own Son in the likeness of sinful flesh . . . [God] condemned sin in the flesh' (Rom 8.3). By the incarnation the Holy One, God's Son, identified himself with us in our alienated, sin-dominated existence. He took human life from a sin-burdened race, breathed our polluted air and shared to the full in the existential situation of a race whose moral wrongness had corrupted its life and its world in manifold ways. Yet from within this situation he responded to the Father in pure love, pure *human* love. The full wonder of this was partly masked during his pre-Calvary life, for much was shrouded in ambiguity for him, as for us.

The passion laid it bare. He was reduced to chaos: tortured and broken in body, desolate and abandoned in spirit. It was supremely ugly, twisted and horrible; 'he had no form or comeliness that we should look at him, and no beauty that we should desire him' (Isa. 53.2). In him were manifested the consequences of hatred. All sin can do is to violate, destroy and kill. He became the place of naked confrontation, where the horror of sin's work was exposed to the holiness of God.

From within these darkest depths, from the utter negation of this sin-marked chaos with which he was so unreservedly identified, he responded to the Father with that unqualified self-giving love which is the holiness of God. He used the very conditions of chaos to express his love: the pain, shame, degradation and loneliness. He responded by the passionate love that thrust towards the Father through the full horror – physical, mental and spiritual – of our alienated condition, and ultimately through death itself, which had been the sign of sin. Jesus in his passion was identified with the chaos which in the Old Testament had been the revelation of what sin is, identified moreover not with some remote biblical chaos only but with the chaos wrought by sin in every generation, including ours. But he is a chaos which, because it belongs to the Beloved Son, the Lover of the Father, is changed from its very roots and made into the language of loving obedience. This is the radically new thing, the unprecedented act of God which brings into being a wholly new situation.

Running through the New Testament is a conviction that in the cross and resurrection of Christ the last things are already present. This is not confined to John. Paul too thinks of Christ's resurrection as the prelude to the parousia, and his conviction is justified even though his time-scale is too short. In the cross of Jesus God has already judged the world. The Crucified One was 'made sin for us' (cf. 2 Cor. 5.21) so that in him 'we might become the holiness of God'; that is, without guilt of his own he accepted solidarity with us in our situation marked by sin in order to change its meaning from the inside and make it the way back into the Father's arms. The 'Come' of God to man has been answered from within this very situation of 'the flesh'[5] by Jesus's response to the Father, 'And now I am coming to you'.

The divine judgement on sinful mankind in the person of Jesus who has identified himself with it can, therefore, be nothing else than the Father's acceptance in love. The judgement is a 'Yes' to all the promises, an irrevocable covenant of love sealed in Jesus's passover. The reality of what has happened is revealed in the resurrection. The solidarity between us and the Crucified holds still between us and the Risen One. We are so implicated that unless by deliberate, sustained refusal we opt out finally, we shall stand for ever within that judgement revealed in Christ's resurrection, a judgement which is love. Our freedom and responsibility are respected and taken seriously, not only in the negative sense that we have the fearful, meaningless power to choose 'anger', but much more positively in that we are invited and enabled to share in the work of human redemption. Good has triumphed, not by any fiction or dodging the issue but by the victory of love in the stronghold of evil. Our intuitions were right after all.

This is why the early Christian preaching, which crystallized in the New Testament, thinks of Christ's resurrection as something like Scene I of his coming in glory. There is a kind of identity between resurrection and parousia, rooted in the person of the glorified Christ. It took a little time and experience for the first generation to realize that the link between the two events did not mean a swift succession, but this realization is already apparent in the later Epistles of St Paul. The resurrection is a once-for-all event in Christ himself; in his members it is both once-for-all event and continuous process. The baptized are already dead to sin and risen with Christ; they walk in newness of life; they are seated with him in the heavenly places. Yet there is a time-lag while the resurrection works its way in them, and through them in the whole of creation. The old order dominated by sin has been judged and condemned, but it has power still and a lease of time.

The risen body of Christ is the seed of the new creation planted within the old chaos. Christ the man is related to the whole cosmos, as is every other human being, by an immensely complicated web of genetic, chemical, physiological, intellectual and cultural ties. But *this* part of the cosmos, the part which is Christ's manhood, is risen and glorified.

The shock-waves go through the whole; every part is affected. His risen body is like a radio-active substance lodged in the heart of the universe.

During this in-between time the Eucharist is the special mode of his presence within creation. The risen Christ is among us and within us, in his physical reality and his Easter power. He is in touch with our physical humanity still destined to die, and through us in touch with the cosmos to which we also are inextricably related, a cosmos doomed to death but containing already the seed of its glory. The Church has to continue to 'do this in memory' of Christ, showing forth eucharistically the death of the Lord until he comes again.[6]

The New Testament apocalypses suggest that convulsions in the old order will precede the final coming. Matthew 24.8 speaks of these chaotic signs as 'the beginning of birth-pangs' (ōdines); the allusion is to Isaiah 26.17; 66.7, and similar passages we have considered in earlier chapters, where 'birthpangs' herald the coming of the messianic kingdom.[7] The birth of the new creation, however agonizing, is certain, because of the resurrection of Christ, the 'first-born from the dead'. A theme found in other parts of salvation history is suggested again here, by Luke's Gospel: 'Now when these things begin to take place, look up and raise your heads, because your redemption is drawing near' (Luke 21.28). When human resources are bankrupt and the situation is desperate, God's gifts are given and his glory is revealed.

The vindication of the holiness and glory of God is the other face of judgement in the New Testament apocalypses. One of the effects of sin is to insulate us, in our condition of 'flesh', with layers of insensitivity to God's holiness. Some layers are peeled away from the saints and mystics, who become incoherent when they try to report what they have perceived of the Holy One. Some passages of Scripture suggest the same experience, notably the descriptions of Isaiah's inaugural vision and of the Transfiguration of Christ. One of the most powerful comes in another part of Isaiah:

> Mankind shall be brought low,
> all men shall be humbled. . . .
> Get you into the rocks and hide yourselves in the ground
> from the dread of the Lord and the splendour of his
>   majesty.
> Man's proud eyes shall be humbled,
> the loftiness of men brought low,
> and the Lord alone shall be exalted
> on that day.[8]

The final coming of Christ must strip away the masks and screens, the insulating layers of triviality and self-deception and the sheer opaqueness of sin which have shielded humankind from the radiant holiness of God. We shall have to undergo the searing experience of repentance and purification by love. That this will be terrifying we have good reason to believe, for exposure to love is no soft option, but the holy and glorious God who will then be manifested is the same God we have known all along the road of history in more hidden ways. He cannot contradict his earlier revelations of himself, and it is in those revelations that we have learned to recognize his glory. Power, majesty and light, certainly; but these are not the heart of the matter. His glory is self-sharing love, endlessly and recklessly poured out.

The final coming must, then, be sheer gift, like the first coming in the incarnation and the manifold comings in grace. The new creation will be alight with God's glory, a glory vindicated as love: unmerited love where we are wholly bankrupt. The old creation is an ikon of the new, but the new is far more glorious, and it is born of forgiveness.

The Church was born of forgiveness in its first creation at Easter and Pentecost; its foundation members were all explicitly forgiven men and women. Even in the earthly phase of its existence, therefore, the Church is both human (from below) and pure gift (from above), but this will be far more true of its eschatological life. The saints who compose it will be those who have come through the great tribulation, forgiven sinners who have washed their robes in the blood of the Lamb; yet at the same time the glorious Church is the new Jerusalem which 'comes down from heaven from God' (cf. Rev. 21.2), pure gift. Creation, old or new, is like that: God gives you to yourself.

Characteristic of divine advents is healing. Israel's Messiah is the Sun of Righteousness who rose with healing in his rays; he claimed the role of the anointed prophet who is sent to bind up the brokenhearted and proclaim liberty to captives; at his coming the eyes of the blind were opened and the ears of the deaf unstopped, the lame man leapt like a hart and the tongue of the dumb sang for joy. His secret presence in our own lives is a source of healing for the wounds that life has dealt us in the complicated situations where we hurt, maim and imprison one another by sin. This healing may take all our lifetime, but it is sure. The Last Judgement will necessarily be a divine healing operation on a colossal scale. Healing and judgement are already very close together in our own experience. Christ's command in the Sermon on the Mount, 'Do not judge', is an injunction not to imprison or destroy one another by our condemning attitudes. God's 'judgement' is not like that; it is a manifestation of his faithful love (condemnation is 'anger' in biblical thinking). If we obey this command we shall be 'perfect, as our Father in heaven is perfect', because when we long to forgive people we release them and heal, and this is what God is doing all the time. His 'Last Judgement' will surely be the same healing work on a universal scale: not all of us in the dock before a relentless judge, but all of us joyfully joining in the great enterprise of affirming, understanding, forgiving and releasing each other, and washing one another's feet. The 'anger' side of judgement, the condemnation, can only be for anyone who refuses to join in the footwashing, the forgiving and the being forgiven.

At the heart of divine judgement, and manifested at last in the final judgement, will be unheard-of, undreamed-of mercy. In Advent the Church prays constantly in the words of a psalm, 'Show us, O Lord, your mercy', and we should consider whether we are prepared to face the implications of such a prayer. It is not for some benevolent, accommodating softness that we are asking, but for the revelation of the very being and glory of God. To be confronted by his self-emptying humility, as he kneels before us begging us to accept his love and forgiveness, as Peter was confronted by a Jesus who knelt before him asking to be allowed to wash his feet, is far more humbling for us than any display of mere power. And yet it will be sheer joy to be so humbled. A prayer in the Roman Missal catches something of the wonder:

> Almighty, everliving God, in your overflowing love for us who pray to you, you go further than we deserve, further even than we desire. Pour out on us your mercy, forgiving those things our conscience dreads and heaping upon us what our prayer does not venture to ask.[9]

Faced with the unveiled truth of our sinfulness and his glory, we shall think it incredible that he could want us, but rejoice beyond measure that he clearly does. George Herbert expressed it with his customary penetration:

> *Man*
> Sweetest Saviour, if my soul
> Were but worth the having,
> Quickly should I then controll
>   Any thought of waving.
> But when all my cares and pains
> Cannot give the name of gains
> To Thy wretch so full of stains,
> What delight or hope remains?

> *Saviour*
> What, childe, is the ballance thine,
>   Thine the poise and measure?
> If I say, 'Thou shalt be Mine,'
>   Finger not My treasure.
> What the gains in having thee
> Do amount to, onely He
> Who for man was sold can see;
> That transferr'd th'accounts to Me.

Man

But as I can see no merit
   Leading to this favour,
So the way to fit me for it
   Is beyond my savour.
As the reason, then, is Thine,
So the way is none of mine:
I disclaim the whole designe;
Sinne disclaims and I resigne.

Saviour

That is all: – if that I could
   Get without repining;
And my clay, My creature, would
   Follow my resigning;
That as I did freely part
With my glorie and desert,
Left all joyes to feel all smart –

Man

Ah, no more: Thou break'st my heart.[10]

God's forgiveness, healing and mercy are much more than an amnesty for man. We do not go back to the primal innocence but through to something better. The garden of the beginning is replaced by the city of Revelation.

In Christ we are all reconciled to the Father, and accepted by the Father in the same love with which he accepts the Beloved Son. Because I am accepted I can learn to accept myself, and on that basis to accept others. In so far as I exclude anyone I shall be self-excluded from the Kingdom, because the Kingdom is the loving, humble, forgiving acceptance of all of us by God. Jesus's parable of the Last Judgement in Matthew 25.31–46 deals with the matter of admission or exclusion, and it is particularly interesting to notice the response of the just: 'Lord, when did we see thee hungry and feed thee, or thirsty and give thee drink? And when did we see thee a stranger and welcome thee, or naked and clothe thee? And when did we see thee sick or in prison and visit thee?' It is a picture not of self-conscious religiosity but of genuine, honest, humble acceptance of people and of the human condition we share. This has been for them, all unknowingly, an acceptance of the Son of Man who has aligned himself with the human condition in all its penury. Such an acceptance is the necessary prelude to hearing the last 'Come' in the lovers' dialogue: 'Come, O blessed of my Father, inherit the kingdom prepared for you from the foundation of the world.'

In Christ not individuals only, nor even our race only, but all creation is reconciled to God. It was the plan of God's love 'through him to reconcile to himself all things, whether on earth or in heaven, making peace by the blood of his cross' (Col. 1.20), and 'that the universe, all in heaven and on earth, might be brought into a unity in Christ'.[11] It cannot be otherwise, because of the outworking of the resurrection from the radiant centre which is Christ's glorified humanity. This means that there must be a redemption of history. At his first coming in the incarnation Jesus took on not simply a human body and a human mind and spirit, but also a human history, inasmuch as he himself became a man within history and lived in solidarity with men and women loaded with all the complexities of heredity, conditioning and sin.[12] The genealogy of Christ in the first chapter of Matthew's Gospel suggests this; that it is not strictly accurate is irrelevant, because it affirms something important about the incarnation. Everything in human history is changed by the entry of the Son of God into it, by his making it his own and taking the weight of it upon his shoulders. He did not affirm the sin as such, but he accepted life from a sin-burdened race and affirmed man, man as he is. This means man in history, man offered grace, man redeemable with his whole web of relationships and experiences. On the principle of the analogy between the various 'comings' of the Lord, this gracious acceptance of us precisely as history-conditioned will be completed at his final coming. The parousia will not simply be the end of history, in the sense that a chapter is closed, and history is discarded and superseded; the parousia must be in some way the affirmation of history, not of its sin but of its goodness through the secret grace of God.

It will be the redemption of history and the bringing of it all to a unity in Christ.

The personal history of each one of us is precious to him.[13] He is more willing to forgive our sins than we are to ask forgiveness, and he is well able to redeem our deficiencies too. We shall not spend eternity kicking ourselves for opportunities lost, grace wasted and love refused. How he can make these things good is beyond our understanding, but in some way the whole of it will be taken up into Christ. Some lines scribbled in the margin of a fourteenth-century manuscript convey an unknown scribe's insight into this mystery:

> He abideth patiently,
> he understandeth mercifully,
> he forgiveth easily,
> he forgetteth utterly.

All the positive things too will be taken up into Christ, to be saved in all their reality and transfigured in him: the love that we have given and received, the moments of aching beauty, the longing and the pain, the laughter and surprise, the plain plodding on. And the redemption of our personal history will be only one facet of the love that redeems all history, purging its sin and saving all the precious memories of the human family. Nothing is lost in him. All the great loves, all the heroism, all the struggle to make life more human, all the wrong turnings people have taken in their search, the times when a light more than human seemed for a while to play over human lives and those lives became legend, the poetry of the particular, the unrepeatable beauty, the fidelity to a vision that demanded all. In Christ all these things will be affirmed and redeemed, to become part of our shared joy, and his.

If all creation is reconciled and redeemed in him, this must include the evolutionary process. We are conditioned, and often led to sin, by those very forces of aggression and self-assertion which brought our ancestors through an immensely long climb to the threshold of humanity, and enabled them, once human, to survive. We are alive today because

161

many, many creatures have died. Domination over other species in competition with ours has required nasty behaviour, and the story is very bloodstained. We do not make a great success of controlling the relevant instincts now. Yet they are part of the creative process, and therefore redeemed. Our bodies, which are the products of this cosmic evolution, are themselves longing for a fulfilment greater than anything life on earth can offer, but explicitly promised by God. In them and through them the cosmos longs, the cosmos that evolved them and groans for its own fulfilment. Very significantly, Paul calls this painful desire birthpangs, and links it closely to the presence of the Spirit within us:

> The created universe waits with eager expectation for God's sons to be revealed. It was made the victim of frustration, not by its own choice, but because of him who made it so; yet always there was hope, because the universe itself is to be freed from the shackles of mortality and enter upon the liberty and splendour of the children of God. Up to the present, we know, the whole created universe groans in all its parts as if in the pangs of childbirth. Not only so, but even we, to whom the Spirit is given as firstfruits of the harvest to come, are groaning inwardly while we wait for God to make us his sons and set our whole body free.
> (Rom. 8.19–23, NEB)

The same intuition of the joyful longing of the cosmos for its eternal spring is present earlier in psalms which lyrically celebrate the coming of the reign of God:

> Let the rivers clap their hands
> and the hills ring out their joy. . . .
> (Ps. 98 (97).8, Grail)

> Let the heavens rejoice and earth be glad,
> let the sea and all within it thunder praise,
> let the land and all it bears rejoice,
> all the trees of the wood shout for joy
> at the presence of the Lord for he comes,
> he comes to rule the earth.

With justice he will rule the world,
he will judge the peoples with his truth.
(Ps. 96 (95).11–13, Grail)

Creation expects its Lover; the Spirit and the Bride say,
'Come'. Playing on the harmonies between his different
advents, the Church uses nuptial imagery to celebrate even
his first coming at Christmas:

> When the sun rises in the morning sky, you shall see
> the King of kings coming forth from the Father,
> radiant like a bridegroom from his bridal chamber.[14]

And again at Epiphany:

> Today the Bridegroom comes to claim the Church, his
> bride,
> for he has washed her sins away in Jordan's waters;
> today the wise men hasten to the royal wedding with gifts;
> today the wedding guests rejoice,
> for Christ has changed water into wine for the feast,
> alleluia.[15]

John's attitude to the Last Things is somewhat different from
that of other New Testament writers. It is not that he ignores
the traditional elements or the usual Jewish time-scheme. In
the Fourth Gospel Jesus speaks of those in the tombs who
will hear his voice and come forth to life or punishment, he
promises to raise up at the last day all whom the Father has
given him, and in the Appendix to the Gospel he indicates
that the beloved disciple may have to 'remain until he comes'
(cf. John 5.28–9; 6.39; 21.22). But John prefers to stress that
the eschatological reality is present here and now in the
person of Jesus,[16] and he interiorizes the realities of the end-
time. The 'coming' of Jesus is his coming into the world
when he took flesh; he does indeed promise to 'come again',
but he is keeping his word already, in the time of the Church,
by coming to his own through his Spirit. The incarnation is
already a manifestation of his glory, and this glory is shown
forth throughout his life by 'signs'. The supreme sign, which

is the exaltation of Jesus and the fullest revelation of his glory, is his 'lifting up' on the cross and his passage to the Father. Christ is to judge all mankind, but this is not postponed until the end of history. The very coming of Jesus, the Light of the World, is already a judgement, a discernment and a crisis. The light shows up what is in us, and we cannot remain neutral; either we shun it and reject it, preferring our own darkness because our deeds are evil, or we come to the light and walk in it, because there is a kinship between it and the truth in our hearts, and because we know our need for forgiveness. The story of the man born blind in John's ninth chapter is almost the Gospel in miniature. Jesus comes to find him; he is a beggar, in need of the light, as we all are. Jesus anoints his eyes with clay, a re-creative act like the creative work of the potter-God in Genesis 2.7, and sends him to wash in a pool named 'Sent', as Jesus too is sent by the Father. The man receives sight for his bodily eyes and gradually opens himself to the light offered to his spirit, finally acknowledging Jesus as the Son of Man: 'Lord, I believe.' His truth and openness to the light contrast throughout with the spiritual blindness of the synagogue officials who refuse the evidence, expel the man, harden themselves in their pride and reject Jesus. They have condemned themselves by their attitude to the light: 'For judgment I came into this world, that those who do not see may see, and that those who see may become blind. . . . If you were blind, you would have no guilt; but now that you say, "We see," your guilt remains' (John 9.39, 41).

Jesus is the Word, and it is the Word of God that judges man, because the Word is God's testimony to himself. To those who receive him he gives, even now, power to become children of God. 'This is eternal life that they know thee, the only true God, and Jesus Christ whom thou hast sent' (John 17.3): eternal life is theirs already because they come to the light, accept the Word, acknowledge their need and are willing to live in his love. The Spirit 'convicts' human beings by his witness to Jesus, and he is the earnest of eternal life already possessed: 'We know that we have passed out of death into life, because we love the brethren. . . . We know that he abides in us, by the Spirit which he has given us' (1 John 3.14, 24).

For John, the drama of the last days is already being played out in first-century Palestine round the person of Jesus. The conflict between light and darkness, truth and lies, love and hate, life and death, is fought out there, and the issue decided. These are the last days.

We have, then, a warrant in the New Testament for trusting some of the intuitions we may have about the Lord's final coming, since John has indicated the analogies between that mysterious future coming and those we already know. Christmas and grace are models for the parousia, and we may expect that certain characteristics of his past and present comings will be found again in that unknown future advent.

Among these 'constant' factors is, first and foremost, the 'sheer gift' quality of any coming of God. He looks for openness, need and thirst; he is gift for the helpless and bankrupt. There is also a strange gentleness about his comings. He does not overwhelm or crush us, but gives in such a way that we can receive him. Even though his final coming will be openly glorious and powerful, it will not blast his creatures out of existence. Closely related to this quality of gentleness is the impression he constantly gives of being very much at home within his own creation, and of making it feel at home with him. As always, there will be intuitive recognition on the creature's part: in the heart of the awe-inspiring, the numinous, the all-holy, is something we have always known.

Nevertheless, those who are to recognize him then will need eyes that see and ears that hear. At the time of his first coming there was plenty of information available before-hand; the whole of the Old Testament experience was God's way of creating an expectation and preparing the chosen people to recognize the Saviour when he should come. Yet his coming confounded most of Israel, because the self-gift of God cannot be simply encapsulated in the words, concepts and images which divine revelation uses to render itself intelligible. Jesus was recognizable only to those prepared to break through, at great personal cost, to the truth; prepared to break through to the Lover who called from the other side of cultural barriers, preconceived ideas, inadequate human formulations and the various moral blocks that make us unwilling to face the light. It seems that the final coming will have an unmistakable quality, but there is still a parallel. We too have plenty of information about it in the New Testament's indications concerning the end-time, in what we know of Jesus's coming in the flesh, and in our experience of his comings in our own lives. But all of these are coloured and shaped by our own limitations, our particular cultural forms and our inadequate understanding. As far as they go, these indications are true, but the reality will transcend them, though without giving them the lie.

Certain conclusions can profitably be drawn. You have to walk in what light you have, not pleading that you must wait until you can see everything clearly before making a decision. You have to leap and choose, and come to the light in practice, by humble response to the truth you see. Only so will you get more light. Initial recognition demands obedience, and obedience leads to further recognition. Even when you have made the radical option to follow Christ and are trying sincerely to walk in his light, you need to keep catching his eye, frequently and deliberately. This is also a preparation for prayer.

Prayer is a response to God's 'Come', and it seems like a response to the invitation, 'Come and be judged now'. It is an exposure to the truth and holiness of God, and it shows up the sin in us, the lie and the unlove. The Word is our judge now, as John suggests, and exposure to it in our daily life and prayer is an anticipation of standing under it at the end. The Letter to the Hebrews presents this aspect of the Word:

> The word of God is living and active, sharper than any two-edged sword, piercing to the division of soul and spirit, of joints and marrow, and discerning the thoughts and intentions of the heart. And before him no creature is hidden, but all are open and laid bare to the eyes of him with whom we have to do.
> (Heb. 4.12–13)

This is an awe-inspiring prospect. But the Word is not an alien, hostile force from without, taking us by surprise, catching us at our worst. If we have tried habitually to live with the Word, to obey it and to be exposed to it in our prayer, we know it already as judging indeed, but also creative; holy indeed, but loving; inexorable truth, but the truth that makes us free in God's presence. Judgement is interiorized now, and we find that it is also healing and peace. In prayer you have to let him know you as you are, let him see you. It becomes the transparency, the vulnerability, of lovers. At least one of the psalmists knew this. Psalm 139 (138) is the prayer of a man who stood under God's gaze in all his incompleteness and imperfection, and found there his utter security and final peace:

> O Lord, you search me and you know me,
> you know my resting and my rising. . . .

All his ways are open to God, wherever he goes God is present, waiting for him in highest heaven and in the grave, at the ends of the earth, in darkness and in light. God's creative gaze was on him before he was born, during the long, slow process which brought him into being. The same eyes are on him now, knowing him, creating him still:

> Too wonderful for me, this knowledge,
> too high, beyond my reach.

This is judgement, but it is not terror. It is transparency to God, and the creature longs for it:

> For it was you who created my being,
> knit me together in my mother's womb.
> I thank you for the wonder of my being. . . .
> (Ps. 139 (138). 1, 2, 6, 13, 14)

Judgement at the end will be a positive, joyful experience. We shall be there in our truth, undefended against the healing, affirming love of our Creator. Surely this is what purgatory is. It may be that we get our purgatory now, in the measure that we allow God to know us, and allow his word to be the two-edged sword for us, even now. The truth is cleansing. John links it very closely with forgiveness:

> If we say we have fellowship with him while we walk in
> darkness, we lie and do not live according to the truth; but if
> we walk in the light, as he is in the light, we have fellowship
> with one another, and the blood of Jesus his Son cleanses us
> from all sin. If we say we have no sin, we deceive ourselves,
> and the truth is not in us. If we confess our sins, he is
> faithful and just, and will forgive our sins and cleanse us
> from all unrighteousness. If we say we have not sinned, we
> make him a liar, and his word is not in us.
>
> (1 John 1.6–10)

We have surrounded the idea of judgement with the
imagery of law courts and punishment, but our experience of
God's judgement and forgiveness of us, obscured though it
partly is by our mortal condition, is very different. It is a
measure of our obtuseness and grudging spirit that we can
still think of God as against us, seeking to condemn. He
could not have done more to convince us that he is more on
our side than we are ourselves, and

> If God is for us, who is against us? He who did not spare his
> own Son but gave him up for us all, will he not also give us
> all things with him? Who shall bring any charge against
> God's elect? It is God who justifies; who is to condemn? Is it
> Christ Jesus, who died, yes, who was raised from the dead,
> who is at the right hand of God, who indeed intercedes for
> us?
>
> (Rom. 8.31–4)

One can almost hear Paul saying it: 'Could *Christ Jesus*? He
least of all!' Judgement by the God who has so loved us is the
redemption of our personal history, and the courteous
invitation to live with a love we have glimpsed but in which
we have scarcely believed. At the end there will be no more
evading it. George Herbert's poem expresses this incompar-
ably:

> Love bade me welcome; yet my soul drew back,
>   Guilty of dust and sin.
> But quick-ey'd Love, observing me grow slack

From my first entrance in,
Drew nearer to me, sweetly questioning
  If I lack'd anything.

'A guest', I answer'd, 'worthy to be here.'
  Love said, 'You shall be he.'
'I, the unkind, ungrateful? Ah, my dear,
  I cannot look on Thee.'
Love took my hand and smiling did reply,
  'Who made the eyes but I?'

'Truth, Lord, but I have marr'd them: let my shame
  Go where it doth deserve.'
'And know you not', says Love, 'who bore the blame?'
  'My dear, then I will serve.'
'You must sit down', says Love, 'and taste my meat.'
  So I did sit and eat.[17]

Prayer is a particularly direct way of living out the Church's reality as the one who waits, keeping vigil for the Bridegroom. It is a night watch. It may not feel like that all the time; but then not all of the Old Testament experience felt like that to Israel. They must have thought themselves in broad daylight some of the time. Looking back, we shall know that this life has been a night-time encounter, like Jacob's with God. Plato says somewhere that to those living in heaven our life on earth must look like the muddy waters at the bottom of the sea.

We live towards death. This realization is joyful and positive, and it makes sense of everything we meet on the way. The seasons of life move onwards, and as you experience increasing age you may be tempted to look back to the spring, or try to halt the summer. But the best is yet to be, and there is the fruitfulness of autumn. John Donne saw all times as God's seasons:

God made sun and moon to distinguish seasons, and day, and night, and we cannot have the fruits of the earth but in their seasons: but God hath made no decree to distinguish the seasons of his mercies; in paradise, the fruits were ripe, the first minute, and in heaven it is alwaies autumn, his

> mercies are ever in their maturity. We ask *panem quoti-*
> *dianum*, our daily bread, and God never sayes you should
> have come yesterday, he never sayes you must againe
> tomorrow, but *to day if you will heare his voice*, to day he will
> heare you. . . . Though in the wayes of fortune, or under-
> standing, or conscience, thou have been benighted till now,
> wintred and frozen, clouded and eclypsed, damped and
> benummed, smothered and stupefied till now, now God
> comes to thee, not as in the dawning of the day, not as in the
> bud of the spring, but as the sun at noon to illustrate all
> shadows, as the sheaves in harvest, to fill all penuries, all
> occasions invite his mercies, and all times are his seasons.[18]

After the fruitfulness of earthly maturity comes, in many
people's lives, the decline and failing of powers, like the
falling leaves and dying landscape of oncoming winter. But
winter is precisely our (northern) approach to another
Advent, and the late autumn of life is our sure, joyful
approach to the greatest personal Advent we have known,
'the last of life, for which the first was made'. It is the time of
trusting readiness for the last 'Come', and God's chance to
prepare us for the last breakthrough, the new birth. This life
is our ante-natal period, and our own suffering is part of the
birthpangs of the new age. Then there will be the recognition
of what the whole of life has been obscurely showing us.
'When he appears we shall be like him, for we shall see him
as he is' (1 John 3.2). Death is our breakthrough to the
fulfilment of the promise hidden in that early invitation,
'Come and see'.

In each of us the destiny of all our race is worked out
personally; through each of us who responds to him
mankind moves towards the Lord of the world to come.
Only after what we, from our restricted viewpoint, call 'the
Last Things' will the story of man with God really begin.
History is short, and we are made for eternity. The interval
for each of us, and even for the human family, is only a 'little
while':

> 'After a little while you will see me no more, but again after a
> little while you shall see me.' This 'little while' of which the

Lord speaks is the whole length of time through which this present age speeds on its course. That is why John says in his First Letter, 'This is the last hour'. . . . The apostles, who then saw Christ in his bodily form, would soon no longer see him as a mortal man. . . because he was about to go to the Father. But his next words, 'Again after a little while you shall see me', are a promise made to the whole Church . . . and the Lord does not long withhold what he has promised. Only a little while, and we shall see him, and then we shall make no requests and ask no questions, because nothing will remain to be desired nor will anything lie hidden to puzzle us. This 'little while' seems long to us while we are still waiting, but when it is over we shall realize how little it was. Meanwhile we should not be sad during this time when what we desire is struggling to birth, for the woman in labour, to whom the Lord compares us, is less sorrowful over her present pain than joyful over the child who is to be born.[19]

Faith means life in the presence of the God who is coming. Joyful already, it is a prelude to joy.

10 The Sacrament of Advent

Late have I loved Thee, O Beauty so ancient and so new; late have I loved Thee! For behold Thou wert within me, and I outside; and I sought Thee outside and in my unloveliness fell upon those lovely things that Thou hast made. Thou wert within me and I was not with Thee. I was kept from Thee by those things, yet had they not been in Thee, they would not have been at all. Thou didst call and cry to me and break open my deafness: and Thou didst send forth Thy beams and shine upon me and chase away my blindness: Thou didst breathe fragrance upon me, and I drew in my breath and do now pant for Thee: I tasted Thee, and now hunger and thirst for Thee: Thou didst touch me, and I have burned for Thy peace.[1]

Journeys end in lovers meeting. Before the final wedding of God with humanity the lovers meet many times, God the giver offering himself, and the human person, who is built to receive, responding. This is what 'grace' is. The encounter of grace is often hidden; but we are bodily creatures, who tend to understand and function best through symbols, which by use of some sensible medium evoke and obliquely express more than can directly be said. The human body and human speech are primary symbols, and through them we communicate. Actions and gestures, special places, times and seasons, the expression of truth and beauty through colour and shape and sound and movement: all of this is a human and spiritual use of symbols. God also, the transcendent Wholly Other, can use them for communication and encounter with us, and when he does they become 'sacraments' in a broad sense.

Sacraments are sacred symbols. They are more than signs giving information (like a notice saying, 'The 7.15 for Edinburgh will leave from Platform 5'), and more than signals stimulating a response (like a red light saying,

'Danger!'). They are the active presence of a mysterious reality which is partly hidden, but partly revealed by the symbol, and they invite participation. Through them God offers and invites; through them a human person responds with his whole being.

Jesus Christ is the great sacrament. He is both God's self-gift and humankind's reply, with the barriers down. In this one place God's desire to give himself has encountered without hindrance the radical openness to God which is man's deepest meaning. Christ is the sheer gift, the unheard-of manifestation of love. The gift of Christ to the world is the primordial grace, and it is the model and possibility for every other gift of God to us. Yet Jesus also focuses mankind's radical openness, attunement and receptivity. He, more than any other, has the capacity to receive God, and we all have it because of him. He is grace offered, but he is also grace accepted. The dynamic grace of 'ordinary' human life has found its supreme manifestation in his life, death and resurrection. In his growth, speech, work and relationships, in his prayer, suffering and joy, in his hope and faithfulness, in his love and courage and obedience, the secret locked into the heart of human life and destiny is made plain. Because this is so, every human being who in his truest moments recognizes God's grace as the deepest meaning in his own life, and is obedient to it, has already implicitly said 'Yes' to Christ, and is linked in fellowship with all others who watch for his coming, and wait for him.

Through human physicality, God meets us. That is not difficult to accept. That it should be in this concrete individuality of Jesus Christ; that here in this one man, localized in history and place, there should be the unique encounter: this is a harder saying. The 'scandal of particularity' has offended the best minds down the centuries; some of the broadest and the most humane have regarded the claim as bigotry. Yet however we reinterpret it, we cannot give it up.

The Church is the visible, bodily presence of Christ the Great Sacrament; the Church, in all its imperfection, is the localized presence of grace offered and accepted in Christ. Christian understanding of how this can be true develops, however. The Second Vatican Council veered away from language about the Church as the one Ark of Salvation for all, though without repudiating that image. To medieval minds who believed the human race to be about 4000 years old, and the inhabited world not to extend very far beyond Europe, it may have still been natural to think of actual membership of the Church as a real possibility for the majority of mankind. We can no longer think so; it is evident that the people who explicitly enter the Church are only a minority. Yet God wills all men to be saved and to come to a knowledge of the truth. The Light which has come into the world enlightens every man; the Word is scattered like seed amid the nations and down the centuries. All who are saved share in the salvation won for them by Christ, whether they know his name or not; and if this is true the Church must in some way matter to them, even if they never have any contact with it in credible form.

The Second Vatican Council preferred to say that the Church is related to them as the sacrament of universal salvation. The Church is the place of visibility, the symbol that partly reveals a reality which though transcending it is yet present in it. The Church is a sacrament which invites participation. Here is the real presence of the saving God; here is grace embodied, but not grace confined.

Israel too was scandalously particular. In the tenth chapter of Genesis we are given a 'Table of the Nations', full of outlandish names; it is a picture, drawn according to the limited knowledge available to the authors, of the scattered and diversified families of mankind. Out of this multitude one man is called, Abraham. The whole strange, scandalous paradox of particularity begins here and runs through the entire Old Testament: the one for the many, the one line whose existence is made possible by innumerable other lines. There are so many not chosen. The far more cultured and intelligent Chinese and Greeks are passed over, though nothing is said, nor can anything be said by the biblical writers, of the presence of the self-revealing God of grace among them. God's election was not meant to be a cause of self-esteem for Israel:

The Lord your God has chosen you to be a people for his own possession, out of all the peoples who are on the face of the earth. It was not because you were more in number than any other people that the Lord set his love upon you and chose you, for you were the fewest of all peoples; but it is because the Lord loves you, and is keeping the oath which he swore to your fathers.
(Deut. 7.6–8)

Not for its own glory was Israel chosen, but to be a covenant-people for the sake of the nations, a sacrament for all mankind of the salvation which was to come. Occasionally, Israel realized it. Particularism was a method in the service of universalism.

The Church too is a luminous sacrament among the nations of that salvation, now given. God's secret grace is never restricted to official channels. It pervades human history and human experience; and all history will be seen as redeemed in Christ at the end. What will be matter for wondering joy to us at his final coming is true now. Human life is pervaded by grace – grace offered and grace accepted – in a million forms. But what is general, pervasive and hidden seeks a point of visibility, and this it finds in the Church, particularly in the Eucharist and other explicit faith-encounters.

Neither for Israel nor for the Christian Church is election a ground for boasting, an opportunity for self-aggrandizement or a claim to privilege. It is a vocation of service to all the others. Israel was the servant-people, though it so seldom remembered the fact, and the Church is the Servant-Church. On the whole Israel's vocation was a very humbling one. The epics and sagas of other peoples glorify their ancestors; Israel's are different, for they glorify the Lord. Israel saw justly when it prayed, 'Not unto us, O Lord, not unto us, but unto thy name give the glory'. This is even truer of the Christian Church: it is the place of embodied grace, of promise and covenant; but its history is stained by every kind of sin and betrayal. It has its epics of holiness, but they are unequivocally attributed to God. Ringing in the ears of its

175

members is the warning, 'To whom much is given, of them much is required'.

In this perspective, Advent is a particular 'sacrament' within the general sacramentality of the Church. In Israel's longing, and then in the transposition of this into the Church's celebration of the 'Come' mystery, there is a poetic, sacred symbol, a sacrament. Just as there was in the ancient world a chosen people for the sake of all peoples, an election of the one man, Abraham, for the sake of all the families of the earth, an exclusiveness for the sake of ultimate salvation for all, one people formed to hear and bear the Word so that all in the end might hear it, so there was an explicit, focused, articulate longing for God in Israel as a sacrament of all men's longing. Israel was a transparent symbol of Everyman's orientation to grace, and of the need, expectancy and waiting of every human being. So too today the Christian celebration of Advent and Christmas through Scripture, liturgy, personal prayer and faith is indissolubly linked with the longing and the grace of every man, woman and child; linked, that is, with the world's Advent. We can dwell as much as we like on the unique, historical birth of Jesus, on his entry into human history at a precise and particular moment with all its concrete circumstances of time and place, persons and a religious culture. In the vividness of the particular is poetry born, and the 'little local infancy' is full of magic. But this particular event is a sign, a symbol, a participative sacrament of his birth in the life of each one of us, and of his coming in human history everywhere and in every age. Ultimately his birth is the sacrament of the divinization of what is human in every aspect of its reality save sin, and of the consummation of this divinizing process at his final coming. We listen to the special, particularized word here, in Advent's promises and in the Christmas good news, in order that we and all others may hear the word throughout our experience. Both particular and universal are necessary. We sentimentalize only if we forget it.

What we are celebrating is God's desire to give himself to man in fellowship, his effective offer of love in Christ, the preparation of mankind by God to receive the gift, and our continuing need to be open to him in our personal, communal and global life. Since Advent is the sacrament of this meeting, it reveals something of both parties concerned. It is a two-way pointer. It is like a luminous area of scriptural poetry and prayer, shedding light to the left upon the truth of the human condition, and to the right upon the mystery of the God who comes. Both man's need and God's giving are illumined: man's need, because there is something about the gift that makes us able to understand the privation. When we have the remedy, we can better diagnose the disease; when we have heard the good news, we can bear the bad; when we have been confronted by the holiness of God, we recognize our sin. And God's giving, because the gift is revealed for what it is by the sacrament of Advent: not some created bounty alone, but God giving himself. Some consideration of the two ends is needed. First, the left.

In human experience today there are elements which constitute a 'hidden Advent'. Some of them are negative, a painful sense of wrongness and need; others are positive aspirations towards or even inner demand for the vision, the possibility, the 'grace' which will change us and our situation. Some are acutely personal, others are felt more keenly in national or international life. The latter kind can often be seen as the former writ large. To enumerate them is not easy; any list is bound to be selective and can soon become tedious. But the following paragraphs give some indications of the world's 'hidden Advent' themes.

The search for meaning and direction is the most fundamental. Existence is fragmented, and there is no basis or framework of agreement about what human life is, where our destiny lies or what is worth striving for. No single coherent system of values commands general assent, with the result that there is disagreement even on ultimate issues, issues of life and death. Ready-made formulae which purport to explain all are felt to be suspect, but no substitute is available and we cannot live without meaning. There is a fairly widespread impression that our civilization has lost its way. To concentrate on immediate issues and short-term goals, forswearing large vistas, seems more honest, yet the sense of having lost direction grows stronger. Many people are aware that there is something wrong with us, but uncertain what our need is.

One effect of this is that many an individual feels great need for personal affirmation, healing and hope. Each of us needs a conviction that not merely life in general, but my life in particular, is worthwhile and has meaning. We need deliverance from self-hate and despair. At the same time, and despite the rampant individualism in today's world, many people are aware that this kind of personal confidence is not to be found in pure solitude. The individual becomes himself or herself through relationship with others, in some form of community. Hence there is a livelier sense of the need for social justice and equitable sharing, and this too is an Advent theme, as in Israel the prophets associated the coming of the Messiah with an era of righteousness between human beings. Another aspect of this search for community living and justice in relationships is the felt need to integrate our highly valued personal freedom with respect for the rights of others. Western society is sure that it wishes to reject totalitarian claims, but this is not enough if we are unsure what we are free for. One of modern man's needs is to rediscover the meaning of adult and growing obedience, the obedience that human dignity demands. We need to learn how to listen responsibly to the Father's word of love in an evolving situation and with other people.

A further widespread intuition is that these needs, both personal and social, can be met only by a right relationship – indeed, a friendship – with that which is beyond, the transcendent. Many are therefore engaged in explicit God-search, the quest for the God of a hundred names. People are more ready to recognize our radical openness to a reality beyond our reach, which while transcending all other human experience can yet make sense of it. We know our need for truth, and are affronted by all the lies fed to us, but many would find it hard to decide on their criterion for truth. Clear and distinct ideas, the methods proper to the empirical sciences, and all cognitive processes in which the aim is to take maximum precaution against error have achieved remarkable success in their own fields; but they do not serve us well if made into a mesh through which everything must pass if it is to be admitted to the status of reality. If we were to exclude all that cannot be handled by our standard scientific techniques we should ruthlessly impoverish human understanding. There is health for the mind in living with divine mystery. We do not master it, but we are invited into it. As we worship it and let it work on us we come no nearer to comprehension; indeed, it seems to grow vaster and more mysterious than ever. But it is light and life for the spirit, and it has a curious way of lighting up everything else.

Not far from this is another hidden Advent intuition: that at the moments in our lives when the transcendent reality (whether we call that 'God' or by some other name) has touched us, we have been most truly ourselves. Moreover, these moments of encounter with the Incommensurable, the Other, the Holy, have occurred within our most human experiences or relationships; perhaps in love, friendship or forgiveness, or in the recognition of unselfish kindness, humble truth and courage. There are some human experiences which are so plainly open-ended that they become 'sacramental'.

Modern society has no adequate resources within itself to cope with guilt. Having learnt a little of the workings of the human psyche we are prepared to recognize the factors that limit our freedom from within, and the manifold forces that condition our behaviour. Yet this awareness has by no means disposed of the problem of guilt, focused or free-floating, personal or collective. Sophisticated modern persons are as much in need as their ancestors of forgiveness. The depth of this need is fathomed by the gift of God in Christ, with a forgiveness which at once respects us by charging us with full responsibility for what we have freely done, and speaks to that in us which can condemn it as wrong and repudiate it. At the same time he offers a chance of free, loving response and friendship, and he heals, re-creates and affirms in us the truest self.

We have dire need of peace. Superpowers with weapons of unimaginable destructiveness are only the outward manifestation of threatening chaos, because the forces which destroy peace are within our own hearts, and we can wreck our civilization unaided by giving them free play. They are greed and grabbing, ruthless consumerism where there should be reverence and stewardship, the habit of preferring our own short-term advantages to the common good for which society exists, a cleverness untempered by wisdom, a spiritual blindness and ubiquitous fear. We need a peace that will heal the divisions within us and exorcize the fear which looks to violence as the only way to maintain ourselves against the threats from without. Fear of death not only hangs over individuals; people are afraid there may be no peace for the generations to come.

At Christmas the promise of peace is freely given: the angels sing, 'Glory to God in the highest, and on earth peace among men', and Christ is called 'the Prince of Peace'. Yet it is a strange peace, not as the world gives, a non-violent gift which soon becomes a prey to the world's violence. The traditional liturgy of Christmas week is full of contrasts: from the peace of Bethlehem to the murder of the Innocents and the martyrdom of Stephen; from the beauty of the light that shines in our darkness to the strange, brooding atmosphere of a murder in the cathedral on Thomas's day. Christ promises and gives a freedom from fear, but not by evasion. He came 'so that through death he might break the power of him who had death at his command . . . and might liberate those who, through fear of death, had all their lifetime been in servitude' (Heb 2.15, NEB). The New Testament says simply that 'Christ is our peace' (cf. Eph. 2.14). He is what he gives, because the peace he gives is the fruit of our reconciliation with God in him. But it is entrusted to us as a task:

> Readiness to pay the price of peace must be found not only in Christ but in the reconciled community itself. This community must continue Christ's atoning work, it must 'complete what is lacking in Christ's afflictions'. When Christ bequeathed the gift of peace to his followers and when as the climax of the beatitudes he commended the

peacemakers, we can see in retrospect that this was not the promise of tranquillity but the invitation to continue a costly work.[2]

Salvation is free, but never cheap, as another wise man has said. But we cannot afford not to afford it.

Peace with God, peace with one another and peace within ourselves have as both condition and result a peace between us and our environment. Materialism is a powerful lure, but we know its inability to satisfy. A violent relationship to things degrades both them and us. The incarnation consecrates bodiliness and all the material reality of the cosmos; it is an affirmation of the dignity of our physical life and our enjoyment of the world, and a challenge to enjoy these gifts responsibly and with gratitude. Frugality and appreciation, gratitude and joy, care and cultivation have not far to grow before they become a search and a need for beauty. We speak of gifted human beings 'creating' beauty, but they cannot simply conjure it out of themselves. It is generated by rightness of life and relationships, and a respect for human beings and the things needed for human life.[3] Some people grow strikingly more beautiful in old age. Life has made them so, and their faces tell a story.

Another obscure Advent theme is our suspicion that the best experiences we have had contain something indestructible. They cannot simply be annihilated. Nor can we.

Our lives, then, are an Advent. The liturgical season of Advent is a sacrament of Everyman's longing, and this is true for believers no less than for everyone else. A believer who is consciously aware of the season, who stands within the sacramental Advent and thus within the light which is meant for all nations, is deeply conscious of the darkness in himself. He is one with the world which searches, knowing in his own life its doubts, confusions, ambiguities, failures and desires. There are unredeemed, pre-Christian areas in the life of every Christian, chaotic elements needing God's creative touch, blind spots and deafness. None of us has completely come to the light or heard the word. We are in the equivocal in-between state that Paul evokes so vividly, the interim Christianity tensed between Christ's resurrection and the final glory, the mixture of 'already' and 'not yet'. But the believer has heard the challenge and the invitation, and sacramentally meets the offer of grace.

Grace is the ultimate meaning, the last depth, the most radical realization of what it is to be human. Whenever a human person lives as he or she would wish to live, transcending self, whenever a person loves and forgives, stands in the truth to his own cost, acknowledges the claims of goodness upon him, is faithful to the end and dies – however confusedly – into the hands of God, there is the event of grace, there is the meeting.

Our ordinary life is the sphere in which the divinizing, transforming gift has free play. The moments when we explicitly acknowledge God by prayer or sacrament are important, certainly; they are vital. But they are not moments of relatedness to God in an otherwise godless existence; rather they are like the tip of the iceberg, the places of transparency, the moments of disclosure. They show us in particular what is true all the time and everywhere. They are manifestations of the holiness that pervades ordinary life, for the whole world belongs to God, and in its strange and various ways is worshipping him.[4]

Some of the Christian Fathers, vividly and loyally aware of their solidarity with their non-Christian contemporaries, spoke of a presence of God's Word among mankind from the beginning. According to Justin, a distinguished philosopher who became a Christian, and was martyred in AD 165, there had been a 'seminal divine Word' scattered among the Gentiles as well as the Word of revelation to the Jews. Those who sincerely sought the truth had some seed-presence within them of the Word who finally became flesh in Jesus Christ. Justin's teaching on this has application in our world today:

> Whenever the philosophers and lawgivers of earlier days expressed accurately what they had truly found out, they did so through their partial discovery and contemplation of the Word. . . . Plato's teachings are not entirely foreign to

Christ's, even though there are discrepancies, and the same is true of the ideas of Stoics, poets and other writers. The divine Word was scattered among them like seed, and each of them spoke truthfully in so far as he saw in it what he could recognize. . . . Together with God, the unbegotten and unutterable, we Christians worship and love his Word, who for our sake became man so that by sharing our sufferings he might also provide healing. All those thinkers were indeed able, albeit dimly, to perceive reality, because in them was a sowing of the inborn Word. But the seed and imitation of the Word granted thus according to one's own capacity is one thing; it is quite another to have communion with the Word and reproduce his likeness in the way made possible by grace.[5]

Where human beings are concerned, 'pure nature' does not exist. Human nature is incurably oriented towards God, so either it is 'impure nature' when not responding, or it is caught up, however obscurely, in the divinizing gift of God in his incarnate Word. The whole of human life and experience and history are penetrated with it. The Kingdom of heaven is like yeast which a woman took and hid in the dough until it was all leavened.

Man's need, man's shaped receptivity and responsiveness, are created by God who desires fellowship with human beings and prepares them for it. He creates them as responsive, and he more than fulfils their hope. This is why Advent, the symbol of the meeting, reveals not only the one who receives but also the Giver. The sacrament of Advent illumines the right as well as the left.

The particular, local Christmas coming points to the mystery of God: to his humble self-giving, his disconcerting glory, the gentleness of his approach and the beauty of all he does. The human body and human speech are primary symbols; when God's Word is enfleshed in a human nature and spoken in human language, that incarnate Word is a luminous, revealing sacrament of the trinitarian relationship of Father and Son. In the human listening of Jesus the Son's listening to his Father's love is truly present, and the trinitarian mystery invites us through the human sacrament. The self-emptying obedience of Christ in his mortal life is a revelation, under the conditions of mortality in a sinful world, of the self-giving which is the glory of the Trinity. The unique beauty of the Christmas mystery is a sign of the beauty beyond, at the point where timelessness intersects with time.

> To apprehend
> The point of intersection of the timeless
> With time, is an occupation for the saint –
> No occupation either, but something given
> And taken, in a lifetime's death in love,
> Ardour and selflessness and self-surrender.
> For most of us, there is only the unattended
> Moment, the moment in and out of time,
> The distraction fit, lost in a shaft of sunlight,
> The wild thyme unseen, or the winter lightning
> Or the waterfall, or music heard so deeply
> That it is not heard at all, but you are the music
> While the music lasts. These are only hints and guesses,
> Hints followed by guesses; and the rest
> Is prayer, observance, discipline, thought and action.
> The hint half guessed, the gift half understood, is Incarna-
> tion.
> Here the impossible union
> Of spheres of existence is actual,
> Here the past and future
> Are conquered, and reconciled.[6]

God was in Christ, reconciling the world to himself, and it was done through cross and resurrection. The basic grammar of God's dealings with us is that of the paschal mystery, and because this is so it is impossible to speak of Advent and Christmas without Easter perspectives opening at every turn. Some of them have been pointed out in earlier chapters: Mary's obedient 'Fiat' at the Annunciation presages Jesus's 'Fiat' as he confronts the passion; his sonship to the Father, present humanly from the moment of his incarnation, has to be worked out in human living until it is made perfect on the cross and revealed in the glory of his resurrection. He inaugurates his vocation as Servant already in the humility of his coming. His human birth is the beginning of that new creation which will be complete in him at his new birth from the dead and shared with us through the gift of his Spirit. The light which pierces the darkness of our Advent is the first radiance of the light of Easter. Christmas is a feast of fulfilment, the preliminary answer to our hopes and desires, but man's desires have to be crucified and rise again in Christ before they can be perfectly fulfilled.

The Advent–Christmas mystery is therefore an overture to Easter, and it orchestrates the central Christian mystery in ways proper to itself, with its own special emphases. The poor rejoice in the promise; into darkness comes God's light; winter is a prelude to spring; the sterile bear the children of destiny; where we are bankrupt, gifts are poured out; the desert blossoms; the Suffering Servant is to be exalted in glory; chaos is the stuff of the new creation; there is good news for the poor, joy out of sorrow and life out of death. All these are embodiments of the central Christian experience, which is paschal. But they find in the sacrament of Advent a lyrical expression of unique beauty.

The ultimate reality celebrated under these symbolic forms is God's desire to communicate himself to us, to give us his love and draw us into union. Isaiah told us the name of the saving God: it is Emmanuel, 'God-with-us' (cf. Isa. 7.14). He is with us where we are, in all the complexity and concreteness of our need, and not merely where we should like to be. Shortly before Christmas the liturgy prays:

> O Emmanuel,
> our King and Lawgiver,
> for you the peoples long
> and you are their Saviour.
> Come and set us free,
> O Lord our God.[7]

All that he asks in order to give himself is our poverty and

185

need, not our sufficiency. The God who is coming is the consummation of our desire.

The 'Come' theme, from whichever end we view it, is about the advances of lovers. For all the real sinfulness, confusion and darkness in ourselves, we do know that pursuing love. Whatever our chaos, however thick our cloud of unknowing, we yet know. This perhaps is part of the meaning of the Church as the Ark of Salvation: we know that we are plugged into the right story, that mankind's longing is not all dreaming and make-believe and wishful thinking. Our hopes are much more than justified, because what is promised is not only a fulfilment of the expectations of our race; it is a gift beyond our dreams, the advent of something radically new and transforming which yet makes sense of the old. The gift is certain, because God is already pledged, already in our world, already Emmanuel. We are irrevocably, unconditionally loved.

Notes

1 Longing for God

1 Isa. 26.17–18. The reference here is probably not to the bringing forth of a personal Messiah, but to the building up of the messianic people by the repopulation of the land. But the imagery is striking, and this passage, along with Isa. 66.7–8, seems to be alluded to in John 16.20–2, with reference to the resurrection of Christ. On this see further below, p. 61.

2 George Herbert, 'The Pulley'.

2 The Risk of Promise

1 Francis Thompson, 'The Hound of Heaven'.

2 Most of Chapters 1–39 in the Book of Isaiah are the crystallization of the preaching of Isaiah of Jerusalem in the eighth century BC. Chapters 40–55 are of a different character, and are usually assigned to an anonymous prophet who lived some 150 years later, in the century of the exile, whose chief work was to speak the Lord's word to his deported fellow-countrymen. Since he wrote in the general tradition of his eighth-century predecessor, he is known as Second Isaiah or Deutero-Isaiah. The remainder of the book, Chapters 56–66, is composite.

3 See the imaginative evocation of this in Rosemary Haughton, *The Passionate God* (Darton, Longman & Todd 1981), pp. 91–2:
'There was some change of circumstance, some condition of challenge, for which existing humanoid responses were inadequate. And "something happened" which we cannot observe, yet which we can imagine without enormous difficulty because it has the same "character" as that familiar experience called falling in love. We can perhaps conceive of it as a moment when Divine Wisdom appeared to a potentially but not actually human creature and presented to that dazed being the face of Beatrice, the face of the one "by whom all things were made". In that moment he and she, what Charles Williams called "the Adam", was indeed made, in the image of love itself, in the exchange of being with God. Love in the potentially human thing leapt to encounter love, in a thrust of passionate response, and the barrier was broken, and human-

187

kind walked in Paradise, knowing all the earth as newborn, which indeed it was, though it had existed for aeons.' To this book parts of the present chapter are indebted.

4 John 3.3. The Greek word here translated 'anew' can also mean 'from above'. John probably intends the double meaning.

5 On the *'anawim* see A. Gelin, *The Poor of Yahweh*, Collegeville, The Liturgical Press, 1964.

6 Exod. 22.27. This is probably one of the oldest texts in favour of the poor in Israel.

7 T. S. Eliot, 'East Coker' II, from *Collected Poems 1909–1962* (Faber & Faber 1963), p. 198.

8 On all the typology of Luke's Infancy Narrative, see R. Laurentin, *Structure et Théologie de Luc I–II*, Paris, Gabalda, 1957, to which this section is indebted.

9 Matt. 1.18–25 suggests the element of pain and misunderstanding which Mary had to endure. It is possibly hinted also by the Matthaean genealogy of Christ (Matt. 1.1–16), where five women are mentioned, breaking the regular pattern: Tamar, Rahab, Ruth, (Bathsheba) the wife of Uriah, and Mary. Commentators ask what these women had in common to rate a mention. The views are summarized by Raymond E. Brown, *The Birth of the Messiah* (Geoffrey Chapman 1977), pp. 71–4. He supports the opinion that '(a) there is something extraordinary or irregular about their union with their partners – a union which, though it may have been scandalous to outsiders, continued the blessed lineage of the Messiah; (b) the women showed initiative or played an important role in God's plan and so came to be considered the instrument of God's providence or of His Holy Spirit' (op. cit., p. 73). A subordinate motif in Matthew's choice may be that the Old Testament women he mentions were either certainly or possibly Gentiles. In this they do not foreshadow Mary, who was Jewish, but suggest that the Messiah was also for the Gentiles.

3 *Winters of the Spirit*

1 Traditional antiphon at the Magnificat, 21 December.

2 The skeletal remains of the Neolithic farming families who settled near Avebury some 6000 years ago show that 'Death came early. Many men were dead by thirty-six, women by thirty, and although some endured in life to the great age of seventy, perhaps as many as half the children died before they were three years of age. Four

people in ten died before they were twenty.' (Aubrey Burl, *Prehistoric Avebury* (New Haven and London, Yale University Press, 1979), p. 81). There were of course many causes of death.

3   Isa. 9.2 (RSV except last word).

4   The author is too.

5   An unpublished poem by Dom Philip Jebb.

6   Num. 24.17. This oracle was interpreted by Jewish tradition in reference to the Davidic monarchy. Besides this Balaam story, two other Old Testament passages loom in the background of Matthew's account of the Magi. In Isa. 60.1, 5–6, Jerusalem is bidden

> Arise, shine; for your light has come,
> and the glory of the Lord *has risen* upon you. . . .
> The wealth of the nations shall come to you . . .
> all those from Sheba shall come.
> They shall bring *gold and frankincense*,
> and shall proclaim the praise of the Lord.

This prophecy has provided colour for Matthew's narrative, emphasizing the Gentile element and suggesting the details about the gifts. The other relevant passage is Ps. 72 (71).10–11, which speaks of the Gentiles' homage to the messianic King:

> The kings of Sheba and Seba
> shall bring him gifts,
> Before him all kings *shall fall prostrate* (Grail).

Christian tradition has seized on this allusion, and transformed the Magi into kings. Cf. Isa. 49.23.

7   See Evelyn Waugh, *Helena* (Chapman & Hall 1940), p. 240:
'"You are my especial patrons," said Helena, "and patrons of all late-comers, of all who have a tedious journey to make to the truth, of all who are confused with knowledge and speculation, of all who through politeness make themselves partners in guilt, of all who stand in danger by reason of their talents. . . . For His sake who did not reject your curious gifts, pray always for all the learned, the oblique, the delicate. Let them not be quite forgotten at the Throne of God when the simple come into their kingdom."'

8   Cf. *Inferno*, Canto vi, 7 ff.

9   Sigrid Undset, *Kristin Lavransdatter* (Picador 1977), p. 204.

10 Deut. 28.2–3. The northern hemisphere is not so privileged after all. True, it has all the magic of a wintry Advent and a winter feast of Christmas, and this is a great sign, as the present chapter suggests. But the north's suffocating wealth partly conceals the

winter, and it scarcely knows the desert. The elemental things are more evident in the southern hemisphere. Australia has desert at its heart. South America and Africa know raging poverty, as do some Australian Aborigines.

11   Shakespeare, Sonnet 97.

12   Sonnet 98.

13   1 Sam. 2.1, 4–5, 7–8. The story of the birth and childhood of Samuel is part of the background to Luke's Infancy Gospel.

14   *The Stanbrook Abbey Hymnal*, revised edn 1974, no. 31, p. 12.

15   This is also the order of discovery and understanding on the part of the first Christian generation. See Chapter 8, pp. 129–30.

4 *Spring and New Birth*

1   Rainer Maria Rilke, *Sonnets to Orpheus*, First Part, xxi. The German text with an English translation, introduction and notes by J. B. Leishman (Hogarth Press 1967), p. 75.

2   John 1.12–14. Some ancient versions read a singular verb here: 'who *was* born, not of blood, nor of the will of the flesh . . .', etc. The reference then would be primarily to Christ's divine birth from the Father, with a possible allusion also to the virginal conception. John's Gospel frequently presents Christ as empowering us to become by grace what he pre-eminently is himself by nature. Because he is the Only-Begotten, we can become children of God by adoption.

3   Ps. 110 (109).3, Grail. On the application of these oracles to Christ, first to his resurrection, then to his baptism, and finally to his human birth, see Chapter 8, pp. 129–30, and note 3 to Chapter 8.

4   Phillips Brooks, 1835–93.

5   Ephrem the Syrian, *Rhythms on the Nativity*, Rhythms 2, 3, 8. Translation adapted from that by J. B. Morris, Oxford 1847.

6   Luke 2.29–32 (NEB with one word altered). It has been suggested that the canticles in Luke's Infancy Gospel (the Magnificat, 1.46–55; the Benedictus, 1.68–79, the Nunc Dimittis, 2.29–32) were taken over by Luke from circles of Jewish *'anawim* who had become Christian. They may have been hymns of joyful praise at the salvation accomplished in Christ, originally rather general in character, adapted and made specific by Luke for the setting he has given them. For this theory see Raymond E. Brown, op. cit., pp. 350–5.

7   T. S. Eliot, 'A Song for Simeon', op. cit., p. 111.

8 See below, Chapter 7, pp. 108–9.

9 The parallel between Jesus and Moses was important in early Christian preaching. Moses (with Elijah) is seen with Jesus at the transfiguration; Jesus, the new paschal lamb, dies at passover time; the Eucharist is the sacrifice of the new covenant; an early title for Jesus in Jewish–Christian circles was 'the Prophet'; Heb. 3.2–6 draws a parallel between Jesus and Moses (though to contrast them). In Matthew's Infancy Gospel the parallel is used as a partial structure for the story, as Matthew's way of conveying who Jesus is. Joseph is a dreamer of dreams, like the patriarch Joseph through whose agency Israel originally went down into Egypt. A later Pharaoh 'who knew not Joseph' attempted to exterminate all the baby boys born to the Hebrews (cf. Exod. 1–2); and similarly Herod slaughters the baby boys at Bethlehem in an attempt to kill Jesus. Moses escaped because his mother put him in a basket on the Nile; Jesus escapes because Joseph is warned in a dream to take him to Egypt. When Moses, by now grown up, fled to Midian to evade the consequences of killing an Egyptian, he remained there until he was told, 'Go back to Egypt; for all the men who were seeking your life are dead' (Exod. 4.19), and so he returned with his wife and children; the holy family remains in Egypt until Joseph is likewise told, 'Go to the land of Israel, for those who sought the child's life are dead' (Matt. 2.20). Their return gives Matthew the occasion to quote Hosea 11.1, 'Out of Egypt have I called my son', a text which literally refers to the exodus. The intertwined motifs of the exodus and of Jesus as God's Son continue in the accounts of his baptism and temptation in the desert.

10 For a fine picture of a sophisticated modern Peter Pan see Iris Murdoch's novel, *A Word Child* (St Albans, Triad/Panther Books, 1977).

11 'Miraculous it is in nature and appearance, the day-spring from on high, the joyous renewal of life, the vision of the new beginning.

> *Piping down the valleys wild,*
> *Piping songs of pleasant glee,*
> *On a cloud I saw a child. . . .'*

P. W. Martin, *Experiment in Depth, A Study of the Work of Jung, Eliot and Toynbee* (Routledge & Kegan Paul, 7th impression 1971), p. 102. Compare also Wordsworth's 'Intimations of Immortality'.

12 J. A. T. Robinson, *The Human Face of God* (SCM Press 1973), p. 41. The author states the need for Jesus's genetic solidarity with us

very forcibly. It is only fair to mention that he sees it as incompatible with a virginal conception, understood in the literal biological sense.

13 According to Catholic theology the divine Person of the Word is, by virtue of his hypostatic union with a human nature, the subject of human experiences. Statements like 'God hungered and thirsted', or 'God suffered on the cross', are therefore theologically exact: he suffered not in his divine nature but in the human nature which was his; it is the person *who* experiences things. With regard to the acceptance of limitations discussed in the text, the same principles apply. There is a kind of humility in God, the infinite model and source of anything we know under that name. God as God cannot be cramped or suffer from limiting circumstances, but he experiences limitations in the human circumstances of Jesus. This is the fact at which poets and saints marvel: Ephrem's *Rhythms* have already been quoted, and there are analogous ideas in the great Latin hymns: 'Thou didst not spurn the Virgin's womb' (*non horruisti virginis uterum*, in the Te Deum; 'from the little confined space of the Virgin Mother's womb' (*virginis matris clausula*, in the *Conditor alme siderum*). At the ante-natal stage of Jesus's life this is divine humility, but not suffering, since womb-life is natural to a child at this stage, and in any case consciousness is not yet awakened. But at later stages, when Jesus was enduring consciously and for the sake of love various cramping situations in his life, as the text of this chapter suggests, there was a wedding in him of the divine and the human will that it should be so, a coincidence of the two loves.

14 Luke 4.17, 18, 21. Cf. Isa. 61.1–3.

15 Contrast the crabbed comment of the Preacher: 'Nothing new under the sun', Eccles. 1.9–10.

16 *Nullis iam polluamur contagiis vetustatis.*

17 *Ab omni subreptione vetustatis.*

5 *Listening to the Word*

1 T. S. Eliot, 'Ash Wednesday', op. cit., p. 102.

2 Traditional Christianity affirms that the two natures, godhead and manhood, each whole and unimpaired, are united in the one divine Person who is God the Son, the Word. That statement was hammered out in the thought-forms of the ancient world, and we have to be careful how we operate with it if we are to be truly faithful. It excludes a 'human person' from the God-man, but

'person' in the metaphysical sense, not in the sense we tend to understand 'personality' today. Most of us think psychologically rather than metaphysically, and we mean by 'person' a centre of human experience, the subject of finite self-consciousness and created freedom. This is essentially part of what being human means to us, and we need to know that Jesus is one with us where we are most human. To believe less is to fall short of the faith of the Church.

3   Caryll Houselander's rhythm, 'Ghosts and Memories', suggests the growing intimation of God's presence in the heart of a child. It would apply *a fortiori* to Jesus:

> Guess who I am?
> Guess who it is
> that loves you –
> you, who were the breaking of spring
> in my heart
> before the beginning of time:
> guess who I am,
> you,
> in the womb
> before the day star
> I have begotten you.

Quoted by Maisie Ward, *Caryll Houselander* (Sheed & Ward 1962), p. 325.

4   This is not to say that the evangelists present Jesus's baptism, and the Father's word to him, as a moment in his self-understanding. This kind of psychological interest is ours, not theirs. The evangelists describe the episode as part of the Good News to *us*; it is their way of telling us who Jesus is. The reflections offered in the present chapter at this point cannot therefore be simply read off the Gospel accounts of the baptism. Their starting-point is the Church's faith in Christ's integral humanity. Since his mind was human it worked like ours, discovering and appropriating the truth, particularly the truth of himself, in moments of break-through and leaps of understanding. The same remarks apply to the consideration of Jesus's temptations in the following paragraph.

5   The three replies are all quotations from Deuteronomy, the book which most of all draws out the meaning of Israel's experience in the desert. Cf. note 9 to Chapter 4, p. 191.

6   Dag Hammarskjöld, *Markings* (Faber & Faber 1964), p. 167.

7   The prophet needed the people as much as they needed him. So today a prophet needs the community's shared faith both to hear and to deliver his message.

8   Cf. Ps. 95(94).8; Heb. 4.7.

9   Cf. Francis Thompson, 'The Hound of Heaven'.

10   Cf. *The Cloud of Unknowing*, ch. 32.

11   Deut. 30.14; cf. Rom. 10.8.

6 *First-born of All Creation*

1   Traditional antiphon at the Magnificat, 17 December.

2   Wisd. 18.14–15, JB. The first three lines of this passage are used in the liturgy of Christmas in an accommodated sense; that is, for their verbal suitability.

3   The principal passages are Prov. 8.1—9.6; Sirach 24.1–29; Wisd. 7.22—8.1.

4   Ps. 51(50).9, 11, 12, Grail. The Hebrew word for 'create' (*bara'*), when used in the active tenses, always has God as subject. It occurs here in Ps. 51, also in Gen. 1.1, 19, and variously in Second Isaiah, always of divine action.

5   Cf. Walter Brueggemann, *The Land* (SPCK 1977), p. 149 and *passim*. This admirable book draws the parallels between wilderness, exile, chaos and flood, and to it the present chapter is indebted.

6   St Gregory Nazianzen, *Oratio 39 in Sancta Lumina*, 16 (Migne, Greek Patrology 36.353).

7   Water is ambivalent, like night and winter. There are two different lines of symbolism in Scripture, both derived from common human experience. For one of these, which predominates in the present chapter, water is a sign of chaos: of the dark negativity of the beginning and of the destructive inrush of the flood. It sweeps away the firm holding-points in human existence, and ultimately life itself. It is a judgement of God upon sinful mankind, as will be suggested in Chapter 9. The sea was a huge menace; Israel never came to terms with it and their nautical enterprises were not remarkable for success. In the Book of Revelation the seer notes thankfully that in his final version of the New Jerusalem 'there was no longer any sea' (Rev. 21.1). According to the other line of thinking, which concerns us in other chapters of this book in connection with the desert, water is part of God's gift in creation, and the source of life for animals and humans. It is the most essential requirement in the desert, where men die without it and

nothing can grow. Water thus becomes a symbol of salvation, implicitly in the exodus traditions and explicitly in Second Isaiah; and for John's Gospel water is the favourite symbol for the gift of the Spirit. It is typical of John's irony that he shows Jesus tormented with thirst on the cross at the moment when in his glorification he becomes the source of the Spirit for mankind. Parched land and human thirst are the sign of man-without-God, and with this 'Spiritless' condition Jesus has identified himself. John is making the same assertion that Paul makes under different imagery: 'God made him to be sin who knew no sin, so that in him we might become the righteousness of God' (2 Cor. 5.21). The living water of the Spirit is given to us in baptism, and 'wells up to eternal life' (John 4.14), a foretaste of the 'springs of living water' (Rev. 7.17) and the 'river of the water of life' (Rev. 22.1) which signify the ultimate sharing of divine life in eternity. There is obviously no contradiction between the two lines of imagery; water was necessary, but in the right place and in suitable quantities. In fact both kinds of imagery appear side by side in Ps. 46 (45), in Second Isaiah (compare 41.18 and 44.3–4 with 54.9), and in the Book of Revelation; just as both desert and watery chaos can stand for man's Spiritless condition.

8   Col. 1. 15–18. In Acts 13.32–3 a sermon attributed to Paul also sees Christ's resurrection as a birth, fulfilling the oracle of Ps. 2 which proclaims the sonship of the Messiah. Rom. 1.4 is similar: the resurrection is like a birth because Jesus is thereby 'designated Son of God in power according to the Spirit of holiness'; i.e., he is established as Lord and has won anew the name that is his from eternity. The image of birth is found also in John 16.21–2 and Rev. 12, but the perspective is different; these passages have been mentioned in Chapter 4, pp. 61–2.

7 Glory Reinterpreted

1   Isa. 42.1–9; 49.1–6; 50.4–11; 52.13—53.12.

2   Isa. 49.3. The word 'Israel' in this text is questioned by some scholars.

3   Wisd. 2.12–20; 5.1–7 may be an updating of the prophecy of the Suffering Servant in Isa. 52.13—53.12 to give it topical relevance. Judaism expected an eschatological prophet, *the* prophet, who would be a final revelation of God's wisdom and would usher in a new age. E. Schillebeeckx in *Jesus: An Experiment in Christology*, Collins 1979, suggests a category of understanding available to

Jesus's contemporaries which would have enabled them to perceive his unique significance: some Jewish circles had united the passages about the prophet in Second and Third Isaiah (especially Isa. 61.1) with a Deuteronomic passage in Exodus about a messenger-prophet in whom God's 'name' would dwell (cf. Exod. 23.20–3), and both of these with the Song of the Suffering Servant in Isa. 53 as updated in Wisd. 2.12–20 and 5.1–7. Thus the great Prophet was a messianic figure already for Judaism; he was expected to live in intimacy with God his Father, to suffer and afterwards to be exalted. If this view is correct it is of great interest and explains how Jesus's understanding of the title 'Messiah' did not correspond to the warrior-liberator expectation current among some of his contemporaries. But the theory is controversial, since it is not certain that the ideas available in Hellenistic Judaism and attested in the Book of Wisdom were familiar to Palestinian Judaism at this time.

4   Mark 10.42–5, parallel to Matt. 20.25–8.

5   John 1.14. John uses the Greek verb *skēnoun*, to dwell or pitch one's tent. Both the idea and the sound of the consonants echo the Hebrew verb *šakan*, which is used in the Old Testament of God's dwelling with Israel, particularly above the Ark of the Covenant in the Holy of Holies.

6   Cf. John's earlier remark, 'As yet the Spirit had not been given, because Jesus was not yet glorified' (7.39).

7   St John Chrysostom, *Hom. in illud, Pater, si possibile est*, Migne, Greek Patrology 51.34–5; translation from Friends of Henry Ashworth, *Christ our Light*, 1 (Riverdale, Md., Exordium Books, 1981), p. 245.

8   See René Laurentin, *Court Traité sur la Vièrge Marie* (Paris, Lethielleux, 5th edn 1968), p. 44 and *passim*. In the light of her involvement with Christ's paschal mystery Mary came to be recognized as the prototype of the Church. It was a slow process, though the parallel and contrast between Eve and Mary were drawn even from the second century. By the Middle Ages the complex typology was fully developed. The unifying element is God's plan of salvation. Eve was a first sketch, a type, and her sinful consent brought ruin. There are two lines of symbolism stemming from Eve: God's plan succeeded in two different feminine anti-types, Mary and the Church, each of whom is a 'new Eve'. Mary resumed Eve's consent, but to welcome salvation. The Church is a new Eve born from the side of the new Adam as he

slept on the cross. Both Mary and the Church can in different ways be called 'Mother of all the living', and so both of them are probably alluded to by St John's significant use of the appellation, 'Woman', at Cana and on Calvary. Mary embodies both Israel and the Church. As she had been the link between Israel and Christ, so by her participation in his Easter she became the first of the Easter disciples.

9   The exception is that related in the Appendix, John 21.

10 Isa. 60.1–3, 5, 11, NEB. It must be admitted that according to the original sense of this passage the gates are open to let the Gentiles bring their riches in for the benefit of Israel. When used liturgically it has a different emphasis.

11 Dom Ralph Wright, 'Messiah'.

8 *Who is This?*

1 St John of the Cross, 'Points of Love', no. 21, from *Spiritual Sentences and Maxims*.

2 Compare the centurion's confession, Mark 15.39.

3 The development of the idea seems to have been this. The Davidic king was proclaimed as God's (adoptive) son at his enthronement, so this enthronement was a figurative begetting; hence the language of Pss. 2, 110, 89, etc. The resurrection and exaltation of Christ were understood by the earliest Christians as his enthronement, so also as a figurative begetting. Later, this was pushed back to his baptism, at which the motif of God's acknowledgement of Jesus as the Son is prominent. Finally it was pushed back further still, by the Infancy Gospels of Matthew and Luke, to his conception and birth. This obviously brings the idea closer to an actual, non-figurative begetting: Jesus is Son of God from the time of his conception by Mary, although the Spirit is never presented as the male partner. On all this see Raymond E. Brown, op. cit. (note 9 to Chapter 2, p. 188), pp. 136–7, 160–1.

4 John 1.1 ff. The same understanding is present in Jesus's prayer as given in John 17.5, 18. Compare also Phil. 2.6–7; Col. 1.15; Heb. 1.2.

5 John 8.58. Cf. John 10.30; 14.9.

6 Julian of Norwich, *Revelations*, ch. 67.

7 *The Cloud of Unknowing*, ch. 9.

8 Ibid., ch. 6.

9 T. S. Eliot, 'East Coker', III, op. cit., p. 200.

10   St Ephrem the Syrian, *Rhythms upon the Faith, Against the Disputers*, Rhythm 4. Translation adapted from that by J. B. Morris, Oxford 1847.

11   St John of the Cross, *Spiritual Canticle*, Annotation to Stanza 23, Second Redaction.

12   The Second Vatican Council, *Dei Verbum*, 8. Translation from W. Harrington and Liam Walsh, *Vatican II on Revelation*, Dublin, Scepter Books, 1967.

13   St Ignatius of Antioch, *Letter to the Romans*, 7.

9 *The Final Coming*

1   Hilaire Belloc, 'The Fire', from *Collected Verse* (Harmondsworth, Penguin Books, 1958), p. 132.

2   Blessed Guerric of Igny, *Sermo II in Adventu Domini* (Migne, Latin Patrology 185.16–17).

3   The principal passages are Matt. 24; Mark 13; Luke 17.22–37; 21.8–36; 1 Thess. 4.13—5.3; 2 Thess. 1.6—2.12; 2 Pet. 3; and much of the Book of Revelation.

4   This kind of statement obviously does not refer to the destiny of any individual Jew, either of Jesus's time or since, with regard to personal salvation in Christ; every member of the human race is chosen by God and called to be saved. But Israel of the old covenant had, as a people, a special election which made it the bearer of mankind's hope and gave it a particular role. This election achieved its purpose in the faithful remnant who accepted Christ, and it has passed from Israel to the Christian Church, which is made up of Jews and Gentiles. In Romans 9–11 Paul wrestles with the problem of how God's apparent rejection of his people is compatible with the promises, and arrives at a wondering contemplation of the divine mercy, which has permitted Israel's collective infidelity to ease the conversion of the Gentiles, but will in time use the Gentiles' obedience to provoke the return of Israel. Even without their former role to play, the Jews are still 'beloved for the sake of their forefathers' (Rom. 11.29), and their reconciliation will be like 'life from the dead' (11.15). If the father in the parable was so delighted at the return of his prodigal younger son, what will be the joy of God and of all the Church when the returning prodigal is none other than the lost elder son, come home to take his rightful place in the family?

5   The 'flesh' in Paul's thought is not the material component of man

as opposed to the immaterial, but the whole man with all his components in so far as he is alienated from God. Man indwelt by the Spirit of the risen Christ is 'spirit' even in his body.

6   In the light of this it is possible to see more clearly what kind of relationship holds between the old and the new. The seed of the new creation is sown within the old before chaos sweeps in; the old order is the matrix of the new thing, but it is more than a mere environment. It is not even sufficient to say that there is organic connection between them, because that could conjure up the image of a parasite, lodged within the lifestream of its host and lethal precisely because of its organic connection. A parasite lives not for its host but for itself, and prospers by sapping the host's life. In the case of the Eucharist the opposite happens: the new feeds the old.

Every analogy limps, and this one must not be overworked, but there are three vital points about the relationship that must be noticed. First, the new is truly representative of the old; there is a genuine continuity or identity between them. Noah's race are not another species but human. The *'anawim* are truly the core of Israel, the 'qualitative Israel'. The Church is a single body formed of the two peoples, Jew and Gentile. Jesus is fully and authentically man and involved with our race. Second, the new is present within the old for the latter's good, out of love. The old creation can attain its own fulfilment only in the new. It is not as though the new thing within its heart were an intruder which the old order could reject, and then go on to find its own perfection. Third, the new creation fully shares in the pains of the old; it does not simply emerge and go scot-free. Noah and his family have a bad time, though they survive it. The *'anawim* suffer intensely in the invasion of Judah and the exile. The Church grieves at Israel's tragedy, notably in the person of Paul who is in anguish for his brethren, his kinsmen by race. This is even more poignant in Jesus himself. Not only does the chaos work itself out in him in his passion, but he agonizes to the utmost over the approaching destruction that will engulf Jerusalem and his people. By the same token, the Church all down the ages is inextricably involved with the world's history and its suffering.

7   The same word is used in Acts 2.24 of Jesus's passion: the birthpangs of death were 'loosed' in his resurrection.

8   Isa. 2.9–11, NEB. This oracle may have referred to some particular intervention of God expected within the prophet's lifetime. There

is no need to interpret it as eschatological in its literal sense. But according to the principles suggested in the present chapter, this particular 'judgement' is a sign of the final judgement.

9 Twenty-seventh Sunday of the Year.

10 George Herbert, 'Dialogue'.

11 Eph. 1.10, NEB. The Greek word *anakephalaiōsasthai* means 'sum up' or 'recapitulate' or 'bring everything together under one head'.

12 Cf. p. 55 above.

13 See the moving evocation of this in Major Scobie's conversation with God before his suicide, in Graham Greene, *The Heart of the Matter*, Book 3, part 2, chapter 2.

14 Antiphon at the Magnificat on Christmas Eve.

15 Antiphon at the Benedictus on the Epiphany.

16 As has been suggested, this element is already present in the Synoptics. The time is fulfilled and the Reign of God is at hand; the Beatitudes are messianic blessings; Jesus is Lord of the Sabbath; his healings and exorcisms are advance experiences of the Kingdom; many parables challenge the hearers to a decision heavy with eternal consequences. But the Fourth Gospel is more explicit.

17 George Herbert, 'Love Bade me Welcome'.

18 John Donne, 'All Times are God's Seasons', from *LXXX Sermons: Sermon II*, published in *The Oxford Book of English Prose*, ed. Sir Arthur Quiller-Couch (Oxford, Clarendon Press, 1940), pp. 168–9.

19 St Augustine, *Tractatus CI in Ioannis Evangelium*, 6 (Migne, Latin Patrology 35.1895–6).

10 *The Sacrament of Advent*

1 St Augustine, *The Confessions*, x, 27. Trans. F. J. Sheed, Sheed & Ward 1944.

2 J. Macquarrie, *The Concept of Peace* (New York, Harper & Row, 1973), p. 22. Professor Macquarrie examines the different notions of what peace is among the great cultures of the world:
(*a*) the biblical idea of *shalom* as completeness, fullness, unity, wholeness; the somewhat similar Russian idea of *mir*, something whole or complete like the world itself; the Sanskrit *santi*, which is spiritual contentment, the profound integration of the inward life of man.
(*b*) the very different Greek notion of *eirēnē*, which is basically a truce, a pause in the hostility which is man's normal state, and the related Latin idea of *pax*, an agreement or compact.

(c) the Chinese *ping*, different from both the above, with its connotations of adjusting, balancing and harmonizing opposing forces; this introduces a valuable note of dynamism into the concept of peace.

The first two groups disagree as to whether wholeness or fracturedness is to be considered the primordial and normal state of man. Biblical thinking, for all its realism about sin, thinks that righteousness is more original than sin. Peace is primordial, but it is also a gift for the eschatological time.

3 I was once privileged to talk to a master-potter in Japan, not a Christian, and to see his workshop. He said that you cannot put beauty into things, nor can you catch it; 'it comes from behind', from God. When you are doing what you have to do and making things man needs for his daily life, and putting your heart into it, the beauty comes. The fire in the kiln, he said, is like God: it changes the things we make, and makes them beautiful.

4 See K. Rahner, 'Secular Life and the Sacraments' in *The Tablet*, 1971, pp. 236–8, 267–8, to which article the two preceding paragraphs are indebted.

5 St Justin, *Apologia II pro Christianis*, 10, 13 (Migne, Greek Patrology 6.460, 465–7).

6 T. S. Eliot, 'The Dry Salvages', op. cit., pp. 212–13.

7 Traditional antiphon at the Magnificat, 23 December.

Index